F. Scott Fitzgerald in Minnesota
Toward the Summit

F. Scott Fitzgerald in Minnesota

Toward the Summit

David Page and John Koblas

NORTH STAR PRESS OF ST. CLOUD, INC.

Dedication

For Diana and Sharon

Library of Congress Cataloging-in-Publication Data

Page, Dave, 1954-
    F. Scott Fitzgerald in Minnesota : toward the summit /
David Page and Jack Koblas.
       176 p. 25.3 cm.
       Includes bibliographical references and index.
       ISBN 0-87839-107-X
       1. Fitzgerald, F. Scott (Francis Scott), 1896-1940—Homes
and haunts—Minnesota. 2. Fitzgerald, F. Scott (Francis Scott),
1896-1940—Knowledge—Minnesota. 3. Fitzgerald, F. Scott
(Francis Scott), 1896-1940—Childhood and youth.
4. Authors, American—20th century—Biography. 5. Authors,
American—Minnesota—Biography. 6. Minnesota—In
literature. I. Koblas, John J., 1942-   . II. Title.
PS3511.I9Z78 1996
813'.52--dc20
[B]   96-34806
                                      CIP

Front cover illustration: Scott Nelson. F. Scott Fitzgerald stands in front of the St. Paul Cathedral (center), Josiah King Monument (far right), and the James J. Hill House (far left).

Back cover photo: John and Dave when they began research for the book (1982). Photo by Tish Foxwell.

Map: Irene Vande Moore

Copyright © 1996 Dave Page and John Koblas

ISBN: 0-87839-107-X

All rights reserved. No part of this book may be reproduced by any means, electronic or mechanical, without the express, written permission of the publisher.

Printed in the United States of America by Versa Press, Inc., East Peoria, Illinois.

Published by: North Star Press of St. Cloud, Inc.
                      P.O. Box 451
                      St. Cloud, Minnesota 56302

Acknowledgments

WE ARE INDEBTED to the Minnesota Historical Society for the support and guidance offered by all the employees and to the many courteous librarians we besieged at the Minnesota Historical Society, the Hill Reference Library, the Minneapolis Public Library, the Duluth Marine Museum, the Duluth Public Library, the St. Louis County Historical Society, the Goodhue County Historical Society, the Red Wing Public Library, and the St. Paul Public Library, especially its Highland Park, Lexington Avenue and Merriam Park branches.

We are also grateful to the following places and persons, some who have passed on, for granting interviews through the years or for giving us access to their facilities and materials: Sister Mary Regina McCabe and the other good sisters of the Convent of the Visitation; John S. Fitch, school historian of St. Paul Academy; Father Clyde Eddy of St. Paul Seminary; Gene J. Marshall of the White Bear Yacht Club; Margery Schneeman of the White Bear Area Historical Society; Ethel Cline, former owner of the Fitzgerald residence at 599 Summit Avenue; Richard McDermott, present owner of 481 Laurel Avenue; the St. Paul Town & Country Club; the St. Paul Seminary; and Peggy Rupp of the Commodore Hotel and University Club.

To the following people, we owe a very special tribute. Although some of their contributions are specifically acknowledged in the footnotes, each in his or her own way shared useful information—memories, research notes, an elusive fact, or perhaps a vital telephone number: Margaret Culkin Banning, Garrard Beck, Mrs. Richard Bertram, Ruth Blake, Mary D. Cannon, Elizabeth Griggs Clark, Robert D. Clark, Rose Snyder Claude, Jill Clayton, Mrs. John Dalrymple, Mrs. Richard Emmet, Jr., Mrs. John Farrington, William Forbes, Jr., Msgr. Francis Gilligan, Carolyn Gilman, Evelyn Glendenning, Benjamin G. Griggs, Vince Guarnera, Theresa Gurney, Lloyd Hackl, Brooks Henderson, Keith Horning, Frank Hurley, Jr., Mr. and Mrs. Norris D. Jackson, Alexandra Kalman, Jeanette Kamman, Helen T. Katz, Mrs. Walter J. Kennedy, Clara Kohler, Pat Labadie, Mr. and Mrs. Andrew LaBarre, Mrs. Herbert L. Lewis, Harry Mackenhausen, Margaret Maclaren, Mrs. and Mrs. George Mairs, Elberta Matters, Marion Matters, Carroll Mattlin, Mrs. Daniel McCarthy, Patrick and Mary L. McQuillan, Judy Medelman, Diane Moellring, Mary Alice Murphy, May Maginnis Murphy, George Muschamp, Thomond O'Brien, William O'Connell, Mrs. and Mrs. Richardson B. Okie, Steve Osmond, Peter B. Phelps, Jack Ramaley, Clifton and James Read, Mrs. Cecil Read, Dan Runyon, Frances J. Sains, Roseann Sanders, Mrs. Carl T. Schuneman, Jr., Barbara Simpson, Philip Stringer, Jean Ingersoll Summersby, Mackey J. Thompson, Jr., Joseph H. Watson, William Westen, Mrs. Perry Wilson, Joseph M. Wise, John Withy, and Jack G. Young, Louis Zelle, and Dr. Mike Zlonis.

Quotes from *The Great Gatsby* are reprinted with permission of Scribner, a Division of Simon & Schuster, from *The Great Gatsby* (Authorized Text) by F. Scott Fitzgerald, edited by Matthew J. Bruccoli. Copyright 1925 Charles Scribner's Sons. Copyright renewed 1953 by Frances Scott Fitzgerald Lanahan. Copyright 1991, 1992 by Eleanor Lanahan, Matthew J. Bruccoli, and Samuel J. Lanahan as Trustee u/a dated 7/3/75 created by Frances Scott Fitzgerald Smith. Quotations from *The Romantic Egoists* are used with the permission of Harold Ober Associates.

Contents

Prologue

IN JULY 1995, a Twin Cities' daily newspaper mentioned F. Scott Fitzgerald in an editorial on the need to preserve St. Paul's Summit Avenue. The writer quoted what he called Fitzgerald's "sour" description of the thoroughfare as "a museum of American architectural failures," then went on to suggest, "F. Scott Fitzgerald wasn't fully objective; he never made the inner circle of the avenue's wealthy."[1]

To begin with, the architectural failure line came from an unpublished sketch in which a visitor to Crest Avenue, obviously a play on Summit Avenue, wonders why his hostess has taken him down the entire length of the road.

"This is our show street," responds the woman.

The very next and last line of the sketch is the separate paragraph: "A museum of American architectural failures."[2] The punctuation clearly suggests it is the guest making the comment, not the native. Because the visitor is named Scott, it is easy to assume that Fitzgerald was trying to view the prestigious street through the eyes of a newcomer, even though he himself was born and lived much of his life in St. Paul until his mid-twenties. And it is just as easy to assume, as the editorial writer did, that Fitzgerald enjoyed making fun of his hometown's "show street."

But a passage in a published story, such as "Winter Dreams," will give readers quite the opposite impression. In this story, the protagonist drives a flapper back from downtown toward the Uni-

". . . many events there [in St. Paul] will always fill me with a tremendous nostalgia."
Letter to Marie Hersey
October 4, 1934

versity Club, which in St. Paul sits on Summit Avenue. He turns toward the residential area:

> The dark street lightened, the dwellings of the rich loomed up around them, he stopped his coupé in front of the great white bulk of the Mortimer Jones' house, somnolent, gorgeous, drenched with the splendor of the damp moonlight. Its solidity startled him. The strong walls, the steel of the girders, the breadth and beam and pomp of it were there only to bring out the contrast with the young beauty beside him. It was sturdy to accentuate her slightness—as if to show what a breeze could be generated by a butterfly's wing.[3]

Besides being incredibly moving poetic prose, this scene offers readers quite a different glimpse—what could only be seen as a positive portrait—of St. Paul's "show street," not something "sourly" said by a bitter outsider, as the writer of the editorial would have us believe.

Such a portrait of Scott as a St. Paul pariah eager to escape a city he believed turned a cold shoulder toward him is surrealistic. We wish to repaint that image in this book. A tour of Summit Avenue reveals that some of the grand homes are architectural failures: massive granite behemoths that resemble asylums for the criminally insane, simple homes with out-of-place additions, and ornate brick structures with coffins on the roof line. Even more importantly, further scrutiny into the history of these homes finds that F. Scott Fitzgerald was a guest, and a welcome guest, in a large number of them along Summit Avenue and in the adjacent city blocks. This neighborhood and its values permeate the great bulk of Scott's fiction, from his short stories to his novels and plays.

According to Fitzgerald's baby book, reproduced in *The Romantic Egoists*, the child's first spoken word, "up," was uttered in July 1897.[4] He may only have been wishing to be carried by his mother, father, or nurse, Mrs. Knowlton, but "up" certainly describes where Fitzgerald would eventually desire to be. He had a great yearning to be admired, first among his Summit Avenue peers, then by his classmates at Newman and Princeton, and finally by the artistic set in New York, Paris, and Hollywood. What we hope to achieve with this book is to celebrate Fitzgerald's close connections to his hometown and the state of Minnesota and show how those connections were worked into his fiction as he wrote his way "up" toward the Summit.

Dave Page & John Koblas
St. Paul, Minnesota, 1996

Notes

1 "Summit Av.," *Minneapolis Star Tribune*, July 9, 1995, 26A.

2 Matthew Bruccoli, *The Notebooks of F. Scott Fitzgerald* (New York: Harcourt Brace Jovanovich, 1978), 247.

3 Malcolm Cowley, *The Stories of F. Scott Fitzgerald* (New York: Charles Scribner's Sons, 1951), 142.

4 Matthew Bruccoli, et al., eds., *The Romantic Egoists* (New York: Charles Scribner's Sons. 1974), 5.

Introduction

SUMMERS SLIP BY QUICKLY IN ST. PAUL, where snow sometimes lingers in shady crannies until May, and frost may whiten lawns in early September. Minnesota youngsters tend to celebrate intensely the few warm weeks of summer. Scott Fitzgerald was no exception. "Played baseball," "played golf," "played tennis," "playing Indian," he recounted in his *Ledger* during the summers of his youth.[1]

Sports were not the only attraction for young Fitzgerald once he was freed from Saturday dance lessons. Any weekend summer afternoon might find twelve-year-old Scott with his friend Sam Sturgis exiting the Orpheum Theater in downtown St. Paul, blinking as they jostled with the rest of the audience into the sunlight. Scott and Sam, their heads filled with fantasies from the matinee, would loiter on street corners, acting out favorite scenes before meandering toward their homes. Fitzgerald portrayed such a convincing drunk that some of his contemporaries told their mothers he must have been sneaking alcohol. Far from minding the reputation, Fitzgerald reveled in his ability to be convincing.[2]

If the boys had not squandered the fare, they would board the Selby Avenue trolley to avoid the steep hike up Summit Hill. The two had not yet been born when a cable car lost its grip and plunged down the incline, killing one passenger and injuring several, so they delighted in the anxiety of the older passengers who feared a repeat of the January 27, 1888, accident.

"There never was a good biography of a good novelist. There couldn't be. He is too many people, if he's any good."
F. Scott Fitzgerald
in M. Brucolli, et al.,
The Romantic Egoists

1

Orpheum Theater, ca. 1905. Razed. (Author's collection)

Selby Hill Tunnel with St. Paul Cathedral in the background. (Photo by David Page)

Even though the cable had been replaced by electric cars and the severe grade had been dramatically decreased by the opening of a tunnel three years earlier in 1907,[3] the climb toward Summit Avenue was the highlight of the ride. Just before the car disappeared into the darkness of the tunnel, Scott would catch a last glimpse of a troika of architectural landmarks that towered over the entrance to the elite neighborhood. These sites still serve as concrete symbols of three very profound influences in Fitzgerald's life and fiction.

The grandest of these icons is the St. Paul Cathedral, begun in 1905 when the Fitzgeralds were living in New York. For Scott, "the new cathedral, immense and unfinished in imitation of a cathedral left unfinished, by accident in some little Flemish town, squatted just across the way like a plump white bulldog on its haunches."[4] Although a bit irreverent, this description captures quite well Scott's mixed feelings about his relationship with the Catholic Church. The first Irish Catholic to become a major American novelist, Fitzgerald eventually developed a "profoundly religious, if confused, sensibility, and that sensibility derived largely from his Catholic experience,"[5] which included impressive Roman Catholic credentials on both sides of his family.

Scott's paternal grandfather, Captain Michael Fitzgerald, was descended from Thomas Gerard, who arrived in Maryland only seventeen years after the first pilgrims came to America. He was an ardent Catholic but nonetheless brought suit against a Jesuit priest who tried to coerce his Protestant wife and children into attending Catholic services. Exiled to Virginia, Gerard started what has been called the first country club in America,[6] an interesting claim to fame for the progenitor of an author who would spend many hours of his life in various social clubs. On a different branch of the Fitzgerald family tree, Thomas Hatton, the brother of a Fitzgerald ancestor and a Protestant, carried with him to Maryland "Acts Concerning Religion," the first formal declaration of religious tolerance in the New World. Hatton's sister-in-law had sailed to Maryland with him, and one of her daughters married Captain Luke Gardiner, a staunch Catholic who kidnapped his wife's twelve-year-old sister in order to bring her up as a Catholic. Gardiner enters the Fitzgerald family genealogy again through Philip Key, the great-grandfather of Francis Scott Key, who settled in Maryland in 1720. (He built his home next to the manor that had belonged to Thomas Gerard.) Key's first wife was the daughter of John Gardiner, Captain Luke Gardiner's grandson. And, of course, Philip Key is Scott Fitzgerald's great-great-great-great grandfather.

Catholicism was also deeply rooted on Scott Fitzgerald's mother's side. Her father, Philip McQuillan, had steamed up the Mississippi River from Galena in 1857 and obtained a job with the grocery firm of Temple and Beaupre. In two years, he had earned enough to open his own small grocery. With a promising future in St. Paul, McQuillan returned to Galena in 1860 to marry his childhood sweetheart, Louisa Allen, and bring her back to St. Paul.

Taking advantage of the increased need for foodstuffs brought about by the beginning of the Civil War in 1861 and the Sioux Uprising of 1862, McQuillan entered the wholesale grocery business and moved the firm into a three-story stone structure in 1862 named after its owner John Prince.

P.F. McQuillan, Scott's maternal grandfather. (Courtesy Minnesota Historical Society)

One of the first things Philip did in his role as rising young businessman was to help found St. Mary's Catholic Church.[7] On November 12, 1865, McQuillan and other prominent St. Paulites, such as Bruno Beaupre, James J. Hill (although not a Catholic, his wife and children were), Henry H. Sibley, and Henry M. Rice, purchased property at Ninth and Locust on which to erect a parish church.

The cornerstone was laid May 20, 1866, and the building was dedicated on July 28, 1867, with The Reverend John Ireland, later to become Archbishop of St. Paul, preaching the sermon. Annabel, the fourth of Philip's children, was the first to be baptized at the new church the next month on August 4.[8] As the children of the area's prominent Catholic settlers grew older, an idea developed to establish a Catholic girls' school. Once again,

St. Mary's Church, 1917. Scott's grandparents were instrumental in establishing this congregation. (Courtesy Minnesota Historical Society)

McQuillan, Hill, Beaupre, and others contributed money to the project, and, in 1873, six sisters of the Visitation Order arrived by paddle wheeler.

Once in their new quarters, the sisters discovered they had no food. "I'd have to be miraculous to make breakfast out o' black coffee an' no milk, bacon and a barrel o' flour and no yeast or bakin' powder," remarked one of the sisters. At that very moment Mollie—McQuillan's daughter who would later give birth to Scott Fitzgerald—and her friend Marie Beaupre came to the convent door carrying a plate of hot biscuits, a dish of butter, and a pitcher of milk. Almost forty years later after a fire gutted the school, the sisters were sitting around the breakfast table when they heard a knock at the door. To everyone's amazement, in marched Annabel Fitzgerald carrying a plate of buns. The nuns looked on in disbelief, remembering long before when her mother had served them in a similar manner. As the young lady passed around the food, she observed: "History repeats itself."[9]

In September 1873, Visitation Convent school officially opened with fourteen pupils, including Mollie and Marie and the

P.F. McQuillan house in Lowertown St. Paul, 397 E. 10th Street, after it had been taken over by Luther Hospital, 1905. (Courtesy of the Minnesota Historical Society)

daughters of James J. Hill, John Prince, and other St. Paul merchants. Philip and his wife, Louisa, called on the sisters quite often, and it was not uncommon to find the sisters taking advantage of the McQuillans' hospitality in their spacious home in Lowertown, the area on the near east side of St. Paul. Complete with a captain's walk on the roof and seashell sidewalks, the McQuillan residence was one of the more fashionable in town.[10]

In 1877, Philip passed away at the age of forty-three, a victim of Bright's Disease. What followed was one of the largest funerals in St. Paul history. The overflow crowd was forced to stand outside during services at St. Mary's Church, the same parish McQuillan had helped to establish. Included among the grief stricken were a group of boys and girls from the Catholic Orphan's Home, "an institution that had no more generous friend than he whose death they met to mourn."[11] The family fortune, estimated at $266,000, was bequeathed to Louisa and the children.

Louisa continued to be active in all aspects of St. Mary's church. In March 1882, she and her daughter Annabel were part of group who presented Father Louis Caillet with a check for $12,000 in order that he might retire the parish's debt. The next year, the two commemorated Annabel's baptism by donating a marble baptismal font and pedestal, which are still in use today.[12]

By the mid-1880s, 130,000 Catholics resided in St. Paul, fully two-thirds of the city's population. The McQuillans' generous support of the Catholic Church insured the Fitzgerald family's high position in this large group. When Louisa's grandson Scott Fitzgerald requested an audience with the pope in 1921, the archbishop of St. Paul, Austin Dowling, wrote him a letter of introduction: "I know his family well, none have merited more of the Church in this city than they have through several generations—staunch, devout, generous."[13]

Fitzgerald was baptized two weeks after his birth by Father John T. Harrison at the original St. Paul Cathedral, located at

Sixth and St. Peter in downtown St. Paul. During his youth, he attended church and visited the Visitation Convent with his mother to recite for the nuns sections from a history of the United States he had begun. His enthusiasm for the Catholic religion at this stage in his life led to an attempt "to convert every neighbor to Roman Catholicism—and they were all staunch House of Hopers! [a Presbyterian Church still standing at 797 Summit]"[14]

During his second year at Newman, an East Coast Catholic prep school, he came under the influence of Father Cyril Sigourney Webster Fay and writer Shane Leslie, both of whom were Catholic converts. With them, Fitzgerald discussed becoming a priest-novelist or, at the very least, writing the great Catholic novel.

Since a priest plays a major role in his hot-selling first novel, which was dedicated to Monsignor Fay and even bears the religious title *This Side of Paradise*, it is difficult not to see obvious connections between Fitzgerald's art and the Catholic Church. However, as Fitzgerald himself matured, he seemed to become at best a closet Catholic. "I am ashamed to say that my Catholicism is scarcely more than a memory," Fitzgerald wrote from St. Paul in 1920 to Princeton friend and classmate Edmund Wilson, but he quickly amended, "no that's wrong it's more than that."[15] By the time Fitzgerald returned to St. Paul the following year with his wife, he had abandoned most of the outward rituals of the church, such as attending mass, but he did have his only daughter, Scottie, baptised at the Visitation Convent in November. As a gesture, it did not go far enough. "St. Paul could forgive Scott everything," said Mary Alice Murphy, the woman who moved into the Fitzgeralds' home on Goodrich after they departed, "except that he didn't go to 12:30 Mass."[16]

Ernest Boyd, a writer who met Fitzgerald in New York after he abandoned St. Paul for good, insisted in 1924 that Scott's Catholicism had not disappeared: there are "still venial and mortal sins in his calendar," Boyd wrote, and "his Catholic heaven is not so far away that he can be misled into mistaking the shoddy dreams of a radical millennium as a substitute for Paradise."[17]

One story, although perhaps apocryphal, is indicative of Fitzgerald's shifting attitudes toward the church. According to Scott, he made his last confession while he was stationed at Montgomery, Alabama, during World War I. The girl he was dating at the time was Catholic, and one Friday afternoon as they were walking past St. Peter's Church, Scott decided it was a good time to seek absolution. After he had been shriven, he persuaded his date that she, too, should confess. The young woman listed a half dozen minor transgressions, then began to stammer. The priest asked if she was finished. ". . . I . . . think so," she replied.

"I fear I shall have to prompt you," the priest insisted.

"Why, Father?"

"Because I heard your young man's confession first."

According to a friend of Zelda's, Fitzgerald was more irritated than amused by the incident.[18]

Despite any growing ambivalence, Fitzgerald himself clearly recognized the important role the church played in his life and literature. In 1928, when telling journalist Charles G. Shaw about his chief early influences, he topped the list with the Roman Catholic Church.[19] Certainly Scott was not merely referring to the few priests who appear in his fiction. In 1926, critic Frances Newman claimed Fitzgerald's short story "Absolution" must

> be a story which meant something definite to its author when he was writing it. The Catholic Church is in its very blood, and in its less magnificent manner, and with its less magnificent soul, it shows an American Catholic boyhood as clearly as James Joyce showed an Irish Catholic boyhood in the earlier chapters of *A Portrait of the Artist as a Young Man*.[20]

For Catholics, the confession scene in "Absolution" can serve as a reminder of their own sweaty mumblings into the fabric screen of the confessional, and for non-Catholics the scene provides insight into the likely source of Fitzgerald's guilty feelings about sex. After the young protagonist in the story, Rudolph, "exhausted the minor offenses" of being mean to an old lady, taking the Lord's name in vain, and feeling so proud that he believed he was not the son of his parents, he broaches "the sins it was agony to tell."[21] After a moment of physical torment, he finally confesses to having immodest thoughts and listening to his friends say "dirty words." Although Father Schwartz responds only briefly to Rudolph's other transgressions, the priest questions the boy for a half page about his sexual dalliances, despite their fairly innocent flavor. "You should have gone," the priest concludes, "you should have told the girl to go."

Another passage often quoted to show Scott's squeamishness about sex occurs in *This Side of Paradise*. After young Amory kisses Myra at the Minnehaha Club in Minneapolis, "Sudden revulsion seized [him], disgust, loathing for the whole incident. He desired frantically to be away, never to see Myra again, never to kiss any one. . . ."[22] Scenes such as this, J.B. Priestly argues, show that "far from being the advocate of sexual licence he was often supposed to be, Fitzgerald was in fact old-fashioned and almost prudish in his ideas about sex. . . ."[23] In truth, the "ebony mark of sexual offenses"[24] blackens many of Fitzgerald's fictional accounts of male-female relationships. Later in the same novel, "temptation crept over" Amory as he and a female companion are getting progressively drunker.[25] Almost immediately, Amory realizes Satan is at work and bolts from the party. The narrator in the 1927 story "A Short Trip Home" shares Amory's experience with the devil. Despite claiming "I'm no moralist,"[26] Eddie thinks the term "sex appeal" is a "wretched phrase" and takes it upon himself to escort a female acquaintance east from St. Paul[27] to prevent her from consummating a relationship that would end in "catastrophe . . . or else the police and a scandal."[28] When he confronts her paramour, the man disappears—spirit like—into "an abyss of darkness and corruption."[29]

A decade later, Fitzgerald's contradictory feelings about sex continued to provide tension in his stories. In "That Kind of Party," a young man, Terrence R. Tipton, plans a gathering during which he engages in kissing games. Tipton, who with his Irish name "is an obvious counterpart of Fitzgerald,"[30] shares the writer's Catholic conscience. In order to get chaperones away from the house during the party, Tipton sends a fake telegram: "He knew . . . he had sinned, and for a time he had walked . . . an alley saying 'Now I lay mes' over and over for worldly mercy. . . ."[31]

It is a short step from associating sex with guilt to casting women as temptresses, and Fitzgerald did not take long to go down that path. Two of his earliest works, "A Luckless Santa Claus" and "The Trail of the Duke" (penned while he attended Newman prep school) are "mildly moralistic pieces in which a rather dim-witted young man is the dupe of a typical Fitzgerald female, a willful and spoiled destroyer."[32] Judy Jones in "Winter Dreams," Gloria Gilbert in *The Beautiful and Damned*, Daisy Buchanan in *The Great Gatsby*, Nicole Diver in *Tender is the Night* and Josephine Perry in the Josephine stories form a Pantheon of Fitzgerald goddesses who derail male protagonists from the track toward righteousness.

Fitzgerald biographer Matthew Bruccoli has correctly noted that it "is impossible to determine the extent to which Fitzgerald's attitudes toward women were shaped by Irish-Catholic Jansenism," a doctrine known for its rigidly puritanical sexual views and misogyny.[33] Clearly, Fitzgerald the man was not as sympathetic toward or understanding of women as he could have been. But even the most destructive of Fitzgerald-the-writer's females are likable. It is the hero's weak will and romantic sentimentality, rather than any inherent evil in the sexually appealing sirens in Fitzgerald's novels and stories, that causes his destruction. Though selfish, most of Fitzgerald's female characters share a remarkable strength of character.

Although Fitzgerald understandably intended to take advantage of the public popularity of the flappers he created in his short stories, critic Joan Allen argues that in his novels (as well as many of his shorter pieces) Fitzgerald attempts to leave his readers with a religious moral: "the vanity of worldly dreams."[34] Jay Gatsby, Dick Diver, and Anthony Patch fail because they desire to make heaven—or at least a version of it—here on earth. Even when Fitzgerald tried to create sympathy for the philistinism of the Patches in *The Beautiful and Damned*, his "moralizing compulsion takes over as the novel becomes a warning prophecy for the Fitzgeralds' own marriage."[35] Gloria and Anthony are *The Damned*, after all, not just *The Beautiful*.

Toward the end of Fitzgerald's life, his Catholic upbringing continued to provide a moral lifeboat: "Sometimes I wish I had gone along with that gang [Cole Porter and Rogers and Hart]," he wrote to his daughter in December 1940, "but I guess I am too much of a moralist at heart, and really want to preach at people in some acceptable form, rather than to entertain them."[36] Critic

Malcolm Cowley went so far as to claim Fitzgerald's "middle-class Irish Catholicism . . . kept him from denying his obligations to his family and his creditors and his talent as an artist."[37] Although it was that same "artist in Fitzgerald [who] required that he participate as completely as his energy and conscience would allow in the abandonment which marked the Roaring Twenties . . . ,"[38] the moralist kept close tabs. "Parties are a form of suicide," he once told an acquaintance. "I love them, but the old Catholic in me secretly disapproves."[39]

At first, the Catholic Church had trouble discerning the "old Catholic" in Fitzgerald and refused to allow his burial beside his parents in St. Mary's Cemetery, Rockville, Maryland. In 1975, William Cardinal Baum, archbishop of Washington, D.C., granted reinterment of both Scott and Zelda. Of the reburial, Cardinal Baum said:

> F. Scott Fitzgerald came out of the Maryland Catholic tradition. He was a man touched by the faith of the Catholic Church. There can be perceived in his work a Catholic consciousness of reality. He found in this faith an understanding of the human heart caught in the struggle between grace and death. His characters are involved in this great drama, seeking God and seeking love. As an artist he was able with lucidity and poetic imagination to portray this struggle. He also experienced in his own life the mystery of suffering and, we hope, the power of God's Grace.[40]

Josiah King statue and St. Paul Cathedral. (Photo by Dave Page)

A second apex of the inspirational architectural triangle is anchored at the Josiah King monument just west of the Cathedral. King's statue, erected in 1903, symbolizes Fitzgerald's love of history and his keen interest in the Civil War.

The inspiration for the landmark developed as a result of the fact that Alexander Ramsey, governor of the three-year-old state of Minnesota, happened to be in Washington, D.C., when news of the bombardment of Fort Sumter reached the nation's capital on April 13, 1861. The next morning, he hurried to the office of Secretary of War Simon Cameron, an old friend, and tendered a regiment for the country's defense. Cameron, who was just leaving for the White House at the time, presented President Abraham Lincoln with Ramsey's offer. Thus, "Minnesota became the first state to offer troops for the Union cause."[41] Josiah King was the first man to volunteer for the unit that became known as the First Regiment of Minnesota Volunteers.

Scott himself tells about his fascination with the Civil War in a 1939 foreword he contributed to Historic Homes of Maryland in which he claimed to be "a native of the Maryland Free State through ancestry and adoption."[42] The "adoption" may have come from his living for several years in and around Baltimore while Zelda was being treated at Henry Phipps Psychiatric Clinic of John Hopkins University. The "ancestry" no doubt arose on his father's side of the family. In his contribution to the book, Scott reminisced about his childhood in Minnesota when he asked Edward

Fitzgerald, who came to St. Paul from Maryland in the 1880s, such questions as: "—and how long did it take [Confederate General Jubal] Early's column to pass Glenmary that day?" (That was a farm in Montgomery County [Maryland, where his father had been born in 1853].) and: "—what would have happened if Jeb Stewart's [sic] cavalry had joined Lee instead of raiding all the way to Rockville [Maryland]?" and: "—tell me again about how you used to ride through the woods with a spy up behind you on the horse."

A year later, Scott Fitzgerald was dead, and though forced to take an indirect path, he eventually was interred in a Catholic cemetery in the same Rockville where Confederate General J.E.B. Stuart captured 125 Union Army supply wagons on June 28, 1863. Recalling the reburial several decades later, Scott's daughter, Scottie Fitzgerald Smith, admitted that it was "appropriate, and pleasing, that my father is buried in an ancient churchyard in Rockville. . . ."[43] After all, Scottie pointed out, her father had a life-long fascination with history. Of even greater importance, his first success as a writer, she claimed, "came with the production in St. Paul of a Civil War play, *The Coward.* . . ."

The Coward was the third of four plays Scott wrote for the Elizabethan Dramatic Club. Named for its founder Elizabeth Magoffin, the club attracted what the press at the time called the "children of prominent St. Paul families."[44] And, as Scottie suggested, *The Coward* certainly brought Scott his first taste of hometown literary fame. Several notices and photos in local newspapers featured Scott. On the reviews he saved in a scrapbook, the young playwright crossed out the "17" in "17-year-old" and penciled in "16," since his seventeenth birthday had yet to come.

The play—in which Fitzgerald acted the role of Confederate Lieutenant Charles Douglas—is about a young man "who feared to don a uniform and fight for the independence of the South."[45] The first night sold out, earning $150 for the Baby Welfare League. From the Y.W.C.A. auditorium, the show moved out to the White Bear Yacht Club, where a crowd of three hundred "was even more enthusiastic than that which witnessed the opening performance. . . ."[46]

Coward was by no means Scott's first chronicled use of Civil War themes. When he was thirteen, his third published story appeared in the March 1910 St. Paul Academy magazine *Now and Then.* "A Debt of Honor" deals with a Confederate sentry who is to be executed for falling asleep on duty. Because of his youth, he is pardoned by none other than General Robert E. Lee. The soldier redeems himself later during the Battle of Chancellorsville by single-handedly capturing a house full of enemy soldiers who are holding up the Rebel advance. Although a bit on the dramatic side, "A Debt of Honor" was considered good enough by the editors of *Confederate Battle Stories* to include it in their 1992 anthology. The Battle of Chancellorsville works its way into another Fitzgerald piece included in his last book of short stories, *Taps at Reveille.* In "The Night at Chancellorsville," a prostitute recounts when she was trapped in a train on the Chancellorsville battlefield while fighting raged outside.

In a June 1911 issue of *Now and Then,* Scott's fourth cataloged work of published fiction again indicates the influence Edward's Civil War tales had on the young wordsmith. Entitled "The Room with the Green Blinds," the story proposes that in 1869 the real John Wilkes Booth was finally killed in Georgia by a man whose son was framed for the murder of Lincoln. Interestingly, that same year, the body of John Wilkes Booth was finally buried in the Booth family plot in Baltimore. Whether or not this similarity of dates was just a fortuitous coincidence with his plot twist, Scott was undoubtedly familiar with Lincoln assassination lore since Edward's first cousin, Mary Surratt, was hanged for complicity in Lincoln's murder. According to Andrew Turnbull (who knew Fitzgerald while the writer lived in Maryland), once Scott had gained prominence, "his parents wanted him to write a book exonerating Mrs. Suratt [sic], but he said she was either guilty or a fool and in neither case was he interested."[47]

Today, the Surratt Society—a Clinton, Maryland, organization—continues to promote research into Lincoln's murder, including theories that Booth was not killed in a Virginia tobacco barn eleven days after Lincoln's death. As early as 1903, newspapers in Baltimore were calling the 1869 burial of Booth a "mock funeral."[48] Edward may have passed on similar ideas to his son, who then formed his own imaginative hypothesis about Booth's demise.

In addition to his father's stories, Scott gained part of the background material from books he perused. The January 1902 entry for his *Ledger* discusses Jack Butler, one of Scott's friends while his family lived in Syracuse, New York, "who had two or three facinating [sic] books about the Civil War. . . ."[49] More importantly, beginning in 1911, local papers such as the *St. Paul Pioneer Press* carried daily accounts of what had happened fifty years earlier during the Civil War as well as weekly excerpts from *Battles and Leaders of the Civil War.*

Throughout the remainder of his life, Fitzgerald continued to be drawn to the Civil War. He continued to study military history while at Princeton,[50] and soon after he dropped out, he visited the battlefield at Sharpsburg, Maryland. Fifteen years later, in 1932, he and Max Perkins planned a tour of Virginia Civil War battlefields.[51] Writing Perkins in 1934, Fitzgerald mentioned that, in a fit of insomnia, he read "an old account of Stuart's battles for an hour or so."[52] In the same missive he also discusses a comic piece he took the trouble to have set by printers at the *Baltimore Sun* in order to make it look like a real article. In this private joke, Fitzgerald claimed Appomattox was a big mistake and General Grant had really meant to surrender to General Lee.[53]

An interesting tribute to another Civil War legend occurs in Fitzgerald's fiction. From 1928 to 1929, Scott worked on a series of stories based upon his St. Paul and prep-school years. He named the protagonist, a transparently disguised version of himself, Basil Duke Lee, a name probably derived from Basil W. Duke, a St. Louis lawyer who rode with his brother-in-law, Confederate cavalry wizard John Hunt Morgan. Duke and Morgan made lasting names for themselves when they raided into Ohio during the summer of 1863. After Morgan died, Duke assumed command and ended the war escorting Jefferson Davis as the latter made good his escape from Richmond in April 1865. Described by a relative as "essentially a man of the seventeenth century, that century in half-armor, torn between chivalry and realism,"[54] Basil Duke was the type of cavalier Fitzgerald would have liked to emulate: a mixture of gentility and bravado.

Although his foray into medieval France with his Philippe, Count of Darkness, stories produced "among the worst fiction Fitzgerald published,"[55] he did not give up on historical settings completely. In one of the last stories he sold, "The End of Hate," published in June 1940 by *Collier's*, Fitzgerald returned once more to his father's Civil War tales for inspiration. Fitzgerald even hoped to sell the story, about a soldier who is hung up by his thumbs, to the movies. "There are two Civil Wars," he wrote Edwin Knopf, an MGM producer, "the romantic . . . [and the] realistic."[56] As of 1940, Fitzgerald argued, no film had captured the real war.

One of the most interesting uses of the Civil War by Fitzgerald was as a defense of his drinking. "To say that my conclusions [about Zelda] have ever been influenced by drink," he wrote his sister-in-law Rosalind Sayre Smith in 1934, "is as absurd as to think that Grant's '64 and '65 campaigns were influenced by the fact that he needed stimulant and used it."[57]

Nearing the end of his life, Scott wrote a letter in August 1940 to his Cousin Ceci (Clara of *This Side of Paradise*) upon the death of her mother, Scott's Aunt Elise (Eliza), who was Francis Scott Key's cousin: "With Father, Uncle John and Aunt Elise a generation goes. I wonder how deep the Civil War was in them— that odd childhood on the border between the states with Grandmother and old Mrs. Scott and the shadow of Mrs. Suratt [sic]."[58] Old Mrs. Scott was Edward's maternal grandmother, Eliza Key Scott. She helped raise Edward, John and Elise after the death of their father in 1855, and her sympathies lay with the South.[59]

For Fitzgerald, the battle between North and South was more than just good inspiration for his fiction: it provided an analogy for his parents and, through them, for the country itself. According to Bruccoli, Scott "became convinced that Edward Fitzgerald had never recovered from the Civil War and that its disappointments had sapped his ambition."[60] Quite naturally, Scott's "financially inept but 'old American stock' father came to symbolize pre-Civil War southern aristocracy while his mother's financially successful but 'black Irish' relatives came to represent post-Civil War northern nouveaux riches."[61] The clash of these two cultures is one of the important themes in many of Scott's most well-known works, including *The Great Gatsby* and *Tender is the Night.* In them, the fathers of Nick Carraway and Dick Diver "act as moral touchstones" while the "heroes are destroyed by the new materialistic society."[62]

A more obvious example of the culture conflict occurs in "The Ice Palace," published the same year as *This Side of Paradise*. After Sally Carrol Happer travels north to meet her fiancé's parents, she finds herself disliking the mother, who is from the North, but getting along with the father, who is from Kentucky. During a dinner party, her betrothed, Harry, expostulates about the superb athletes and great financiers from the Midwest, but a French professor paints a different picture by insisting that "the Northern races are the tragic races—they don't indulge in the cheering luxury of tears,"[63] a reminder of Sally's reaction at her hometown cemetery where she tells Harry that even "when I cry I'm happy here."[64] On the ride home from the party, Sally Carrol cannot help but tremble as Harry kisses the tip of her ear with his "cold lips."[65] When later she becomes lost in the ice palace, she discovers the truth behind the professor's remark: "You'll never cry any more," she thinks to herself, because "all tears freeze up here."[66] She takes the next train South, where the boys "couldn't support a wife," but where "a certain amount of charm and assurance could be taken for granted. . . ."[67]

After Fitzgerald's death, Amy Loveman pointed out in the *Saturday Review of Literature* that he "played no little part in the social history of our country,"[68] a remark that would have flattered Fitzgerald. But it is as a chronicler rather than as a maker of history that readers through the ages have come to appreciate the talented author. As early as 1925, one of Scott's heroes, H.L. Mencken, called Scott a "social historian,"[69] a label much more attuned to what Fitzgerald hoped to accomplish within his art.

The third apex of the triangle rests at the James J. Hill house the most imposing residence on Summit. A National Historic Landmark, this thirty-two-room mansion was begun in 1887 and cost $280,000 to build. It contains thirty-five fireplaces, eighteen bathrooms, a ballroom, and a two-story art gallery with a skylight roof.

James J. Hill house, 240 Summit Avenue. (Photo by Dave Page)

Born in 1838 in Ontario, Canada, Hill came to St. Paul in the mid-1850s and took a job as a clerk at a warehouse on the Mississippi River. He was eventually able to convince Canadian friends to help him purchase the troubled St. Paul and Pacific Railroad in 1878 and make its name a reality by thrusting it across the continent to the Pacific Ocean. Hill gobbled up smaller lines and turned them into the Great Northern Railroad. By keeping his steel-ribbon empire headquartered in St. Paul, he did more for the growth of the city than any other individual and, thus, inspired Fitzgerald's art.

In Scott's first novel, *This Side of Paradise* (1920), the hero, Amory Blaine, discusses the futility of creating interesting fiction from the subject of business: "Nobody wants to read about it, unless it's crooked business. If it was an entertaining subject they'd buy the life of James J. Hill."[70] Toward the end of the novel, during a paean for nationalization of industry, Amory states: "we'd have the best analytical minds in the government working for something besides themselves. We'd have . . . Hills running interstate commerce."[71]

Another well-known reference to Hill occurs in *The Great Gatsby*. After Gatsby's death, his father tells Nick that if "he'd of lived he'd of been a great man. A man like James J. Hill. He'd of helped build up the country."[72]

The most important portrait of Hill, however, comes from "Absolution," the brilliant short story created from a section Fitzgerald cut from *Gatsby*. Carl Miller, the protagonist's father in the story, works as a freight agent for Hill. "His two bonds with the colorful life were his faith in the Roman Catholic church and his mystical worship of the Empire Builder, James J. Hill. Hill's was the apotheosis of that quality in which Miller himself was deficient . . . [He grew] old in Hill's gigantic shadow. For twenty years he had lived alone with Hill's name and God."[73]

Just as Carl Miller lived in the shadow of James J. Hill, Scott's father lived in the shadow of P.F. McQuillan. "If it weren't for your Grandfather McQuillan, where would we be now?" asked Mollie when Edward brought his family back to St. Paul 1908 after losing his job in New York.[74] Panicked by the firing, Scott thought "Dear God, please don't let us go to the poorhouse; please don't let us go to the poorhouse."[75] From that moment on, Edward was a broken man, Fitzgerald recalled in a 1936 interview. "He was a failure the rest of his days."[76] Despite Edward's lack of success, his son's relationship to Hill was more social than that of Scott's fictional creation. Mollie's sister, Aunt Annabel, was maid of honor at the wedding of one of Hill's daughters, and Scott attended parties at Maryhill, the home Hill built adjacent to his own for his son Louis.

From the monumental residence of James J. Hill to the St. Paul Seminary on the Mississippi River, Summit Avenue continues to be one of the most impressive residential boulevards in the entire United States. It would be difficult for anyone not to be awed by the architectural display. Whether or not Scott Fitzgerald was more enamored of the wealth that Summit Avenue and the Hill home represented than the average person continues to be a matter of conjecture, but he admitted in a 1928 interview that the "wealthy middle-west" was one of the chief early influences of his life.[77] Fitzgerald himself got into the debate about his worship of money in 1936 when Ernest Hemingway made his comment about "poor Scott Fitzgerald and his romantic awe" of the rich in his short story "The Snows of Kilimanjaro." Scott fired off a note to Hemingway saying "Riches have never facinated [sic] me, unless combined with the greatest charm or distinction."[78]

Whatever the case, for many—if not most—scholars, Scott Fitzgerald's fiction provides a fascinating study of money and those who possess it. *The Great Gatsby,* one critic writes, shows a "passionate attraction to the phenomenon of wealth."[79] But to be fair to Fitzgerald, in novels like *The Great Gatsby, Tender is the Night,* and *The Beautiful and Damned* and short stories like "Winter Dreams" and "The Rich Boy," money does not buy happiness. "Let me tell you about the very rich," Fitzgerald offers in the latter story. "They are different from you and me. They possess and enjoy early, and it does something to them, makes them soft where we are hard, and cynical where we are trustful, in a way that, unless you were born rich, it is very difficult to understand."[80]

"But Scott wasn't only a man who better than anyone else wrote about the rich," John O'Hara summarized in 1945. "All he was was our best novelist, one of best novella-ists, and one of our finest writers of short stories."[81]

Notes

1 *F. Scott Fitzgerald's Ledger: A Facsimile* (Washington, D.C.: A Bruccoli Clark Book, 1972), 162-163.

2 A. Turnbull, *Scott Fitzgerald* (New York: Charles Scribner's Sons, 1962), 25.

3 Virginia Brainard Kunz, *St. Paul: The First 150 Years* (St. Paul: The St. Paul Foundation, Inc., 1991), 53.

4 Matthew Bruccoli, ed. *The Notebooks of F. Scott Fitzgerald* (New York: Harcourt Brace Jovanovich, 1978), 245.

5 Joan Allen, *Candles and Carnival Lights: The Catholic Sensibility of F. Scott Fitzgerald* (New York: New York University Press, 1978), xiii.

6 Scottie Fitzgerald Smith, "The Colonial Ancestors of Francis Scott Key Fitzgerald," *Maryland Historical Magazine,* Winter 1981, 363-364.

7 The Rev. James M. Reardon, *The Church of St. Mary of St. Paul,* 1935, 11.

8 *A Century of Service to God and Man: A Brief History of the Church of Saint Mary of St. Paul, Minnesota, 1867-1967"* N.P., n.d.

9 "Sr. Mary Helen Tells the Story of the Visitation of St. Paul," *Vision,* Spring 1978, n.p.

10 A photograph of the home does not appear to show a seashell walk. That particular detail may have been an elaboration concocted by

Fitzgerald. See Marion Matters, "Grandmother's House: F. Scott and the Riddle of the McQuillan Residence," *Grand Gazette,* April 1976, 2-3, for an excellent discussion of the subject.

11 "Dust to Dust," *St. Paul Pioneer Press,* 13 April 1877, 4.

12 The Rev. Reardon, *The Church of St. Mary,* 18.

13 André LeVot, *F. Scott Fitzgerald : A Biography* (Garden City, New York: Doubleday & Co., Inc., 1983), 9.

14 Beth Kent, "Fitzgerald's Back in Town," *The Grand Gazette,* August 1973, 7.

15 F. Scott Fitzgerald, *The Crack-Up* (New York: New Directions Books, 1945), 254.

16 Mary Alice Murphy. Interview with authors. River Falls, Wisconsin, 23 April 1984.

17 Arthur Mizener, *The Far Side of Paradise* (Boston: Houghton Mifflin Company, 1951), 66.

18 Sara Mayfield, *Exiles from Paradise: Zelda and Scott Fitzgerald* (New York: Dell Publishing Co., Inc., 1971), 75.

19 Matthew Bruccoli and Jackson Bryer, eds., *F. Scott Fitzgerald: In His Own Time* (New York: Popular Library, 1971), 283.

20 *Ibid.,* 372.

21 Malcolm Cowley, ed., *The Stories of F. Scott Fitzgerald* (New York: Charles Scribner's Sons, 1951), 162.

22 F. Scott Fitzgerald, *This Side of Paradise* (New York: Charles Scribner's Sons, 1970), 14.

23 J.B. Priestly, "Introduction," *The Bodley Head Scott Fitzgerald: Volume One* (London: The Bodley Head, 1963), 8.

24 Cowley, *Stories,* 161.

25 Fitzgerald, *Paradise,* 112.

26 F. Scott Fitzgerald, *Taps at Reveille* (New York: Charles Scribner's Sons, 1935), 284.

27 The setting is evident from Fitzgerald's references to such local landmarks as Seven Corners.

28 Matthew Bruccoli, ed., *The Short Stories of F. Scott Fitzgerald* (New York: Charles Scribner's Sons, 1989), 381.

29 *Ibid.,* 388.

30 Allen, *Candles,* 10.

31 Jackson R. Bryer and John Kuehl, eds., *The Basil and Josephine Stories by F. Scott Fitzgerald* (New York: Charles Scribner's Sons, 1973), 6.

32 Allen, *Candles,* 31.

33 Matthew Bruccoli, *Some Sort of Epic Grandeur: The Life of F. Scott Fitzgerald* (New York: Harcourt Brace Jovanovich, 1981), 79.

34 Allen, *Candles,* xiii.

35 Bruccoli, *Epic Grandeur,* 155.

36 Fitzgerald, *Crack-Up,* 305.

37 Cowley, *Stories,* xxii.

38 Allen, *Candles,* 88.

39 *Ibid.*

40 *Ibid.,* 144-145.

41 "April, 1861: Minnesota Goes to War," *Minnesota History,* March 1961, 213.

42 Bruccoli, *In His Own Time,* 158.

43 Smith, "Colonial Ancestors," 374.

44 Matthew Bruccoli, et al., eds., *The Romantic Egoists: A Pictorial Autobiography from the Scrapbooks and Albums of Scott and Zelda Fitzgerald* (New York: Charles Scribner's Sons, 1974), 19

45 *Ibid.,* 18.

46 *Ibid.,* 19.

47 Turnbull, *Scott Fitzgerald,* 6.

48 Michael Kauffman, "Historians Oppose Opening of Booth Grave," *Civil War Times Illustrated,* June 1995, 28.

49 *Ledger,* 156.

50 John Kuehl, ed., *The Apprentice Fiction of F. Scott Fitzgerald* (New Brunswick, New Jersey: Rutgers University Press, 1965), 34.

51 Matthew Bruccoli, *Fitzgerald and Hemingway: A Dangerous Friendship* (New York: Carroll & Graf Publishers, Inc., 1994), 161.

52 John Kuehl and Jackson Bryer, eds., *Dear Scott/Dear Max: The Fitzgerald-Perkins Correspondence* (New York: Charles Scribner's Sons, 1971), 203.

53 Bruccoli, *In His Own Time,* 236.

54 Dee A. Brown, *Morgan's Raiders* (New York: Konecky & Konecky, 1959), 28.

55 Bruccoli, *Epic Grandeur,* 388.

56 Matthew Bruccoli, ed. *A Life in Letters: F. Scott Fitzgerald* (New York: Simon & Schuster, 1995), 430.

57 Matthew Bruccoli and Margaret Duggan, eds., *Correspondence of F. Scott Fitzgerald,* (New York: Random House, 1980), 374.

58 Andrew Turnbull, ed. *The Letters of F. Scott Fitzgerald* (New York: Dell Publishing Co., Inc., 1966), 439. Grandmother was Cecilia Scott who married Michael Fitzgerald. Old Mrs. Scott was Eliza Key, Fitzgerald's connection to his namesake, Francis Scott Key.

59 Bruccoli, *Epic Grandeur,* 11.

60 *Ibid.,* 15-17.

61 Kuehl, *Apprentice Fiction,* 35.

62 *Ibid.,* 35.

63 Cowley, *Stories,* 73.

64 *Ibid.,* 66.

65 *Ibid.*, 73.

66 *bid.*, 80.

67 *Ibid.*, 74.

68 Bruccoli, *In His Own Time*, 475.

69 *Ibid*, 349.

70 Fitzgerald, *Paradise*, 219.

71 *Ibid.*, 273.

72 F. Scott Fitzgerald, *The Great Gatsby* (New York: Scribner Paperback Fiction, 1995), 176.

73 Cowley, *Stories*, 164.

74 Bruccoli, *Epic Grandeur,* 23.

75 LeVot, *F. Scott Fitzgerald,* 6.

76 *Ibid.*

77 Bruccoli, *In His Own Time*, 283.

78 Bruccoli, *Dangerous Friendship*, 191. After the story appeared in August 1936 issue of *Esquire,* the line was changed to read "poor Julian" in subsequent reprints.

79 J. Fetterley, "Introduction: On the Politics of Literature," from *The Resisting Reader,* 1977, in D. Herndl and R. Warhol, eds., *Feminisms: An Anthology of Literary Theory and Criticism* (New Brunswick, N.J.: Rutgers University Press, 1991), 385.

80 Cowley, *Stories*, 177.

81 John O'Hara, "Introduction," *The Portable F. Scott Fitzgerald* (New York: The Viking Press, 1945), xiv.

Chapter One

"Up"

*"1897 Feb. The child
laughed for the first time."*
The Ledger

FRANCIS SCOTT KEY FITZGERALD was born in a three-story brick six-plex at 481 Laurel Avenue in St. Paul, Minnesota. Built just three years earlier, the San Mateo Flats were a suitably fashionable residence for the daughter and son-in-law of the former P.F. McQuillan, one of St. Paul's more prosperous businessmen. The attending physician, Dr. Benjamin H. Ogden, resided at 546 Holly Avenue, just a few blocks southwest of the Fitzgerald apartment, a proximity that ensured at least a little comfort to the expectant mother. The author-to-be took his first breath around 3:30 P.M. on September 24, 1896. He weighed a healthy ten pounds, six ounces. Four days later the birth certificate was filed at Ramsey County Court House.

The Mollie McClinthan on the birth certificate was actually Mollie McQuillan. In her mid-thirties at the time of Scott's birth, she had matriculated at the Convent of the Visitation and broadened her horizons even further by traveling to Europe four times before her marriage. Despite her educational advantages, she was an undiscerning reader. As such, Mollie was romantically inclined but found herself with few suitors. Her mother, Louisa, was content to rest quietly at home and did not make any efforts to integrate her five children into St. Paul society. Although not shy, Mollie lacked the vitality that could make up for her oval face, twisted smile and disconcerting green eyes.

Baby Fitzgerald in front of his birthplace, 481 Laurel, 1987. (Courtesy Minnesota Historical Society)

Dedication plaque at 481 Laurel. (Photo by Dave Page)

19

481 Laurel today. (Photo by Dave Page)

Without marital prospects as she approached her thirties, she began dating Edward Fitzgerald. A gentleman in every sense of the word, Edward was medium in height, wore a crisp beard, dressed elegantly, and possessed great personal charm. He attended school at Georgetown University in Washington, D.C., for a period, but never graduated. Instead, he drifted west to secure his fortune, stopping for a time in Chicago before making his way to St. Paul. Though his Southern metabolism was not suited to the physical or business climate of the Midwest, Mollie was attentive, then, after several years of courtship, she grew determined. According to local gossip, the two were married in early 1890 when Mollie threatened to jump into the Mississippi River unless he proposed.[1] The wedding was held in Washington, D.C., where Louisa kept a home. Governor William R. Merriam of Minnesota attended the reception.[2] The couple honeymooned in Europe, then returned to St. Paul, where Edward presided over the American Rattan and Willow Works, a furniture manufacturer located near his late father-in-law's grocery firm.

In 1895, Edward and Mollie were living at 79 Mackubin, a short walk from the apartment at 286 Laurel to which Louisa had moved after selling her Lowertown mansion. Despite Edward's less than stellar financial position, the Fitzgeralds moved into an elegant three-story row house at 548 Portland, just one block off Summit Avenue, where Scott was conceived. Before Mollie gave birth to her first son, disaster struck. Her two girls, ages one and three, died in an epidemic. "I wonder sometimes if I will ever have any interest in life again," Edward wrote his mother, "perhaps so but certainly the keen zest of enjoyment is gone forever."[3] After his father's demise in 1931, Scott claimed that Edward managed to rally for his son's sake: "I was born several months after the sudden death of my two elder sisters and [my father] felt what the effect of this would be on my mother, that he would be my only guide. He became that to the best of his ability." In 1934, Fitzgerald used an identical tribute to the protagonist's father in *Tender is the Night:* "Dick was born several months after the death of two young sisters and his father, guessing what would be the effect on Dick's mother, had saved him from a spoiling by becoming his moral guide. He was of tired stock yet he raised himself to that effort."[4]

Mollie did not leave a record of her feelings, but her son would later link the tragedy to his eventual career: "Well, three months before I was born, my mother lost her other two children and I think that came first of all although I don't know how it worked exactly. I think I started then to be a writer."[5]

Fitzgerald's struggle for success in the arts certainly may have derived from his parents' ambitions for him. Even though he was a second cousin three times removed, Mollie and Edward's son was named after Francis Scott Key, the author of "The Star-Spangled Banner." His parents' stretch to make a connection to a distant relative has not gone unnoticed by literary scholars. French biographer André, Levot, for example, claims that the Fitzgeralds and their son "would make a lifelong point of [Scott's] relationship with Key,"[6] However, when Mrs. Knowlton, the nurse, introduced the newborn during an October 1896 outing to Lambert's Notions Store at the corner of Laurel and Mackubin, many of his admirers may not have recognized the name Francis Scott Key. At the turn of the century, most people would have considered "America" ("My Country 'Tis of Thee") to be the "national hymn." First performed in 1831 or '32, "America" grew in popularity throughout the Civil War.

While "The Star-Spangled Banner" gained prestige during the Civil War as well, "Hail, Columbia" continued to be the song played for visiting dignataries. Despite the efforts of the Grand Army of the Republic for some sort of official recognition for Key's song, nothing happened until 1892 when Colonel Caleb Carlton ordered the song to be performed during functions at Fort Meade, an obscure military reservation in South Dakota. Eventually, Carlton convinced Governor Hastings of Pennsylvania to establish the same custom among that state's militia. Carlton next had an interview on the subject of a "national air" with Secretary of War Daniel E. Lamont, who issued an order in 1894 requiring Key's song to be played at every Army post during evening retreat. The Navy did not follow suit until 1907. When President Wilson proclaimed "The Star-Spangled Banner" the country's national anthem in 1916, Scott was attending school out East. Congress did not make it official until 1931, nine years after Fitzgerald had left St. Paul for the last time.

Even if the baby's namesake did not strike a familiar chord, Mrs. Knowlton was sure to find plenty of curious neighbors at the commercial intersection just half a block west of the Laurel Avenue apartment. Philip Stringer, one of Fitzgerald's eventual classmates, remembered Lambert's as a place children would stop to purchase candy and supplies on their way to and from "Old Webster," an elementary school on the northwest corner of the intersection. Mrs. Lambert was one of the most respected women in the neighborhood and her husband, John, was well liked, even if he had a reputation for "pinching a little liquor from time to time."[7] At Lambert's or William Kane's Grocery (located on the same intersection), someone was sure to fuss over the Fitzgeralds' first son.

The baby developed normally, crawling for the first time and getting his first tooth by the following May. Despite a vigorous start to life, baby Fitzgerald was soon plagued by colic and then by colds. Just before Christmas in 1897 he fell prey to a bronchitis attack that was serious enough to call a specialist. Since the doctor's advice was not followed, according to Fitzgerald's *Ledger,* "the child pulled through."[8] A similar joke was used early in *This Side of Paradise* when Amory falls ill with scarlet fever and physicians are consulted: "However, blood being thicker than broth, he was pulled through . . ."[9]

Despite the light tone of Fitzgerald's *Ledger* entry, the death of Mollie's first two children could not have been far from

Louisa McQuillan house, 623
Summit Avenue, ca. 1910.
(Courtesy the Minnesota
Historical Society)

Louisa McQuillan house today.
(Photo by Dave Page)

her thoughts. Even after Scott's recovery from illness, his mother
was faced with another crisis of sorts: the very real possibility of her
husband's bankruptcy. The financial situation of American Rattan
and Willow Works was precarious at best. As early as 1894,
Edward wrote to his brother John explaining that he was "not in a
position" to send him a Christmas remembrance.[10] At such times,
the presence of Louisa McQuillan was a financial as well as psy-
chological boost.

In 1893 Grandmother McQuillan had invested some of
her legacy in property on Crocus Hill. She purchased six lots
between Summit and Portland on the west side of Dale for a total
of $35,000 from nurseryman William West. She sold a lot and a
half on Summit to St. Paul lawyer William T. Kirke for $6,000 in
1895 and soon after began construction on her Victorian home on
the northwest corner of Summit and Dale.[11] In early 1897, Louisa
moved out of her Laurel Terrace apartment and took up residence at 623 Summit Avenue. Even though the stone house was

modest by Summit Avenue standards, at last the McQuillan family had gained a foothold on St. Paul's "Show Street."

In stark contrast to the McQuillan success story, American Rattan and Willow Works closed its doors for the final time the following year, some five years after depression had struck in 1893. With a wife and child depending upon him and no capital with which to start another business, Edward began to look for other employment. In April, he secured a job as traveling salesman for the firm of Procter & Gamble and shuffled his family off to Buffalo, New York.

Mollie and Scott returned to St. Paul for a reunion with her mother in August 1899. (Mollie was about half-way through her fourth pregnancy.) Grandmother Louisa was still residing in her home on Summit Avenue, but Scott was too young to develop any lasting impressions of his hometown. He noted in his *Ledger* that his "first certain memory" was the sight of his sister Annabel howling on a bed. She was born in July 1901 after Edward had been transferred to Syracuse. The baby Mollie had carried to Minnesota died at birth in January 1900, the third infant mortality suffered by the Fitzgeralds.

During their decade-long stay in New York, either because of the whims of Edward's employer or by personal preference, the Fitzgeralds continued a pattern of frequent moves they had established in St. Paul, going from this hotel to that apartment. With Edward's income supplemented by Mollie's money, the family was able to achieve a standard of living higher than might have been expected from a soap salesman's salary. Mollie took advantage of the situation to spoil Scott by spending winters with him in Washington, D.C.; sending him to Orchard Park, New York, when he caught another cold; packing him off for summer camp in Canada; and vacationing with him in the Catskill Mountains.

Besides being pampered by an indulgent mother during the years he spent out East, Scott developed a slight preference for his Maryland relatives to those in Minnesota. In 1903, he was ribbon-holder at the wedding of his cousin, Cecilia, whose mother, Eliza Delihant, gave him his "first taste of discipline. . . ."[12] Cousin Ceci would remain a life-long correspondent of Scott's, and her brother Thomas Delihant, a Jesuit, was for a time one of his heroes.[13]

The Eastern hiatus came to an abrupt end in March 1908 when Edward was terminated by Procter & Gamble. The decision he made to return to St. Paul and survive by nibbling at the edges of the McQuillan fortune cost him considerably in terms of the goodwill with which he would be treated by the hundreds of scholars interested in the life of his son. But at the age of fifty-five, Edward was in a position, like it or not, that did not force him to a more self-sufficient route. Thus, in the summer of 1908, he brought his family back to the Summit Avenue neighborhood he had left a decade earlier.

Notes

1 Joan Allen, *Candles and Carnival Lights: The Catholic Sensibility of F. Scott Fitzgerald* (New York: New York University Press, 1978), 3.

2 Matthew Bruccoli, *Some Sort of Epic Grandeur: The Life of F. Scott Fitzgerald* (New York: Harcourt Brace Javanovich, 1981), 13.

3 Andrew Turnbull, *Scott Fitzgerald* (New York: Charles Scribner's Sons, 1962), 7.

4 André Levot, *F. Scott Fitzgerald: A Biography* (Garden City, New York: Doubleday & Company, Inc., 1983) 7.

5 F. Scott Fitzgerald, *Afternoon of an Author* (New York: Charles Scribner's Sons, 1957), 184.

6 LeVot, *F. Scott Fizgerald,* 3.

7 Philip Stringer. Interview with authors. St. Paul, Minnesota, 1 March 1984.

8 *F. Scott Fitzgerald's Ledger: A Facsimile* (Washington, D.C.: A Bruccoli Clark Book, 1972), 152.

9 F. Scott Fitzgerald, *This Side of Paradise* (New York: Charles Scribner's Sons, 1970), 6.

10 Bruccoli, *Epic Grandeur,* 13

11 Marion Matters, "Grandmother's House: F. Scott Fitzgerald and the Riddle of the McQuillan Residence," *Grand Gazette,* April 1976, 3.

12 Andrew Turnbull, ed., *The Letters of F. Scott Fitzgerald* (New York: Dell Publishing Co., Inc., 1966), 439.

13 Bruccoli, *Epic Grandeur,* 18.

Chapter Two

St. Paul Academy
The First Year
1908 to 1909

NOT LONG AFTER THE VISIT of her daughter and grandchild in 1899, Louisa McQuillan sold her Summit Avenue mansion, barely two years after she had it built. She took temporary shelter at the Aberdeen Hotel on the southwest corner of Dayton and Virginia.[1] Both the Aberdeen and the nearby Angus were considered two of St. Paul's finest hotels, and many upper-class patrons would reside in one of the two inns while waiting for more permanent lodgings.

In 1901 Louisa left the Aberdeen to take up residence at 472 Holly, but by 1903 she and the her family were back at the Aberdeen, where they would remain for another two years. In 1905 she returned to the Laurel Terrace rowhouse, this time occupying an apartment at 294 Laurel, a few doors down from where she had lived previously. (She called this building home the remainder of her life, passing on in 1913.)

When the Fitzgeralds returned to St. Paul in 1908, Louisa McQuillan took Scott (and possibly Annabel) under her wing at the rowhouse while Edward and Mollie moved in with Dr. John F. Fulton and his family. The Fultons, fairly prominent in St. Paul society, gladly opened their doors at 239 Summit to their friends Mollie and Edward. Mollie eventually secured a position for Edward as a wholesale grocer, hoping he could earn enough to reunite his family under one roof. He kept samples of rice, coffee and dried apricots in a roll-top desk that sat in a corner of his

"After a month he began to realize the full extent of his unpopularity. It shocked him. One day after a particularly bitter humiliation he went up to his room and cried."

"The Freshest Boy"

Laurel Terrace, residence of Louisa McQuillan, at 294 Laurel. F. Scott Fitzgerald lived here in 1908. The building is now owned by the McQuillan family. (1982 photo by Dave Page)

brother-in-law's real estate office, but any sales he made were more an attempt to avoid the embarrassment of not working than to make a living. There was more than enough McQuillan money to cover everyday expenses.

Scott was away from his parents, even if only a few blocks, for the first time in his life. Thrust into a society that had only recently developed far enough to be able to judge people by their social and business connections, Scott Fitzgerald knew he possessed some disadvantages. Edward, in spite of his aristocratic manners and dapper appearance, had failed to make a name for himself in business, and Mollie, who could claim a relationship with one of St. Paul's most respected families, was often the target of gossip because she lacked the very things Edward possessed. One childhood companion of Fitzgerald recalls that "Scott's mother was not really accepted socially even though from a well-off family. . . . She was rather frumpy—with her skirts dragging in the dirt, and her hair coming unpinned and falling down behind. She just didn't know how to dress."[2]

Another acquaintance remembers that, after calling on a friend, Mollie wrote a note expressing the belief she had forgotten something when she returned home. "I think I left 'something' on the bureau in the room in which we visited," the note read. "I would appreciate if you would go check." Then she added the postscript "p.s.—I just found it" and mailed the missive anyway.[3]

Nonetheless, Scott had a knack for ingratiating himself into almost any group. In no time at all, many children of St. Paul's

Finch house, 245 Summit Avenue. (Photo by Dave Page)

elite—H.L. Hersey, the lumberman; Charles W. Ames, president of West Publishing Company; and C. Milton Griggs, the wholesaler—found the attractive young man emerging as an equal, if not a leader. His bright ideas rolled off a glib tongue, for Scott relished any amount of limelight, but he could also be a good listener.[4] Admire him or not, the children soon realized that here among them was a genius of sorts, a bit odd perhaps, but certainly gifted. He developed a friendship with Arthur Foley and was soon playing with the other neighborhood youngsters in the barn behind the Foley residence at 236 Summit.

He had not been in St. Paul very long when Scott encountered Atlanta beauty Violet Stockton, a summer visitor of her aunt, Mrs. Finch. Scott fell hopelessly in love with her. Fitzgerald had experienced flirtations while living in Buffalo, but any memories of former belles faded at his first sight of his fellow newcomer. Naturally, he was not the only boy in the area to be affected by Violet's charms. His friend Jack Mitchell, who resided at 251 Summit, right next door to Violet's aunt, introduced Scott to his pretty neighbor. Although a year older than Scott and rushed by Mitchell as well as Arthur Foley, it was Scott, the leader and inventor, who made the best impression on her. For Violet's amusement, Fitzgerald developed a game called "Indians," which, as the name implies, involved dividing up the neighborhood children into two groups who would then "shoot" at each other with croquet mallets.[5]

Foley and Mitchell made no attempt to conceal their admiration for Miss Stockton. As might be expected from boys their age, they showed their affection by sneaking up on Violet and snipping a lock of her hair. Scott's initial attempts to win Violet were less childish, and he made a good first impression. Through friends, Scott learned that Violet thought him to be polite and cute. She even told Harriet Foster that she liked Scott's teeth so well she wished they were hers. However, Violet did note Scott's short temper and superior airs.[6]

St. Paul Academy, 25 North Dale. F. Scott Fitzgerald attended school here when his family returned to St. Paul in 1908. (Photo by Dave Page)

Eventually, Fitzgerald joined with Jack Mitchell to make off with Violet's diary, which she called "Flirting by Signs." Violet was understandably furious, stormed back into her aunt's house, and slammed the door. Fitzgerald retreated to his grandmother's and brooded over the incident. When Violet called to ask for some form of reconciliation, Scott hung up on her. Now it was Scott's turn to feel remorse. He rang up Violet, and she agreed to come out to play with the gang. The children gathered behind the Schulzes' home at 226 Summit Avenue, which used to stand directly across from the Cathedral. Theodore Schulze, Sr., was a shoe wholesaler, and Scott was a frequent companion of his children—Katherine "Kitty" and Theodore. As the rest of the children gossiped while they overlooked the St. Paul skyline, Scott and Violet sat a little apart. Their infatuation was probably painful for Kitty since she also had a crush on Scott.

Scott asked Violet if she had called him a "brat" and told Archie Mudge she wanted her picture, ring and lock of hair returned. She assuaged all his fears by telling him that Mudge was a liar and a scamp. At that point, Eleanor Mitchell rushed up to them hysterically complaining that her brother Jack was teasing her, so Violet walked her home. Eventually, the relationship cooled as Violet tossed Scott aside in favor of Arthur Foley. However, when she left St. Paul on September 24, Scott's twelfth birthday, she did give him a box of candy. It was the last he heard from her.

Violet would live on, however, in Fitzgerald's Basil cycle of stories under the name of Erminie Gilbert Labouisee Bibble of New Orleans. Miss Bibble is the heroine of "He Thinks He's Wonderful," "Forging Ahead," and "Basil and Cleopatra," although in the latter story, another of Fitzgerald's sweethearts, Ginevra King, probably provided part of the inspiration.

Griggs house, 365 Summit Avenue. (Photo by Dave Page)

All of Scott's affairs were not of the heart that fall. He played football with friends and entered St. Paul Academy. The yellow-brick edifice stood at the corner of Dale and Portland on property once owned by Louisa McQuillan. This private preparatory school was an outgrowth of the Barnard School for Boys, established in 1891. When Scott attended, the facility was so small that it was forced to hold commencement exercies in the Masonic Hall on Laurel near Mackubin or the Unity Church at Mackubin and Holly.[7]

Edward had still not managed to reunite the family, but by this time he and Mollie were living at the Aberdeen Hotel. Mollie continued to push her child socially by having him recite for guests portions of book projects he had begun in Buffalo. On other occasions, she would have him sing. Scott always performed well, but felt he did not have much of a voice.[8] School was not much more to his liking. His grades were mediocre, and he was reprimanded for writing in the margins of his texts. He talked too much, and "endured the humiliation of seeing the school paper, the St. Paul Academy *Now and Then*, print in 1909: 'If anybody can poison Scotty or stop his mouth in some way, the school at large and myself will be obliged.'"[9]

In spite of his antics, two of his instructors recognized a spark in the young man. "Pa" Fiske and C.N.B. Wheeler (the latter would eventually become the school's headmaster) encouraged Scott in his writing endeavors. Still, Scott recognized that the best route to popularity lay in athletics, and he tried out for the Academy football team. He did not become a hero—that role was reserved for others—but he did enjoy playing enough to take part in pick-up games in the vacant lot next to the house belonging to the Griggs at 365 Summit. Benjamin Griggs was a friend of Scott's, and he, Cecil Read and others would frequently gather at the Griggs' home after school and on weekends to talk and keep in shape for the Academy athletic teams.[10]

Throughout the winter, Scott continued his quest for physical prowess by visiting the Y.M.C.A. He boxed with Egbert Driscoll, swam in the pool, and sat in the sauna.[11] He also developed the life-long habit of reading in bed after hours. If he could not make the grade in sports, at least he could read—and eventually write—about them.

In April, Louisa went abroad, and Mollie and Edward moved into her apartment to be with their children. They had been separated for almost a year.

Notes

1 Marion Matters, "Grandmother's House: F. Scott and the Riddle of the McQuillan Residence," *The Grand Gazette*, August 1973, 3.

2 Mrs. Richard Emmet, Jr. Letter to authors, 29 March 1979.

3 Philip Stringer. Interview with authors. St. Paul, Minnesota, 1 March 1984.

4 Benjamin Griggs. Interview with authors. St. Paul, Minnesota, 10 April 1976.

5 In his *Thoughtbook* (Princeton, N.J.: Princeton University Press, 1965), Scott listed the participants as Betty and Archie Mudge, Betty, Harriet and Roger Foster, Eleanor and Jack Mitchell, Dorothy Greene, Marie Hersey, Kitty Schulze, Wharton Smith, Adolph Schelle, Arthur Foley, Violet and himself.

6 The Violet Stockton affair is convered quite extensively in Scott's *Thoughtbook*.

7 St. Paul Academy archives.

8 Andrew Turnbull, *Scott Fitzgerald* (New York: Charles Scribner's Sons, 1962), 22.

9 Matthew Bruccoli, *Some Sort of Epic Grandeur: The Life of F. Scott Fitzgerald* (New York: Harcourt Brace Jovanovich, 1981), 25.

10 Benjamin Griggs. Letter to authors, 13 April 1976.

11 *F. Scott Fitzgerald's Ledger: A Facsimile* (Washington, D.C.: A Bruccoli Clark Book, 1972), 163.

Chapter Three

An Inchoate Gatsby 1909

In the summer of 1909, Scott rushed toward his teens with mixed feelings. His first year at St. Paul Academy had been less than successful and, like the vast majority of youngsters his age, he felt his parents were a burden. Under the heading "Jan 1909" in the Ledger which he started keeping in his early twenties, Fitzgerald complained about having "*to sing for company—God!*"[1]

In an often-quoted reference about his parents made in a 1926 letter to his editor Max Perkins, Fitzgerald filled his pen with poison instead of ink. "Why shouldn't I go crazy? My father is a moron and my mother is a neutoric, half insane with pathological nervous worry. Between them they haven't and never have had the brains of Calvin Coolidge."[2] The entire letter is a bit tongue in cheek ("If you see anybody I know, tell 'em I hate 'em all..."); nevertheless, the observation about Edward and Mollie is quite damning. Ironically, French biographer André, LeVot misidentifies the passage as coming from correspondence dated September 15, 1936. In that missive, Scott actually praises his mother, who had just left him enough of a legacy to ameliorate his immediate financial problems: "She was a defiant old woman, defiant in her love for me in spite of my neglect of her, and it would have been quite in her character to have died that I might live."[3]

Fitzgerald also praised Edward after the latter's death in 1931: "I loved my father—always deep in my subconscious I have referred judgments back to him, what he would have thought, or

> "I wouldn't ask too much of her," I ventured. "You can't repeat the past.
>
> "Can't repeat the past?" he cried incredulously. "Why of course you can."
>
> The Great Gatsby

done."[4] The passage appears almost verbatim in Fitzgerald's 1934 novel, *Tender is the Night*: "Dick loved his father—again and again he referred judgments to what his father would probably have thought or done."[5]

A short year later, he was not quite so kind. In 1935, he and a friend visited the Asheville, North Carolina, boarding house made famous by Thomas Wolfe in *Look Homeward, Angel*. Mrs. Wolfe still managed the place, and although both the Wolfes and the Fitzgeralds were Southern families who had failed at "keeping up appearances" after the Civil War, Scott found nothing positive in the link and was particularly appalled by Julia, Tom's mother. "Poor Tom! Poor bastard!" he lamented upon leaving the house. "She's a worse peasant than my mother!"[6]

Scott was not alone in his negative evaluations of his parents. Although Scott's St. Paul friends and their families found him to be "bright and alert, friendly and lively, well-mannered,"[7] his parents were a different matter. Elizabeth (Betty) Ames Jackson, whose family home Scott immortalized in "The Scandal Detectives," recalled that neither her parents nor the parents of her husband socialized with Mollie or Edward. "Mrs. Fitzgerald used to walk by the house and she always looked drab and dreary to me. We'd say 'How do you do,' and that was the end of it. My impression was that life at home was dreary for Scott."[8] Betty's husband, Norris, thought of Edward as a "recluse" who "knew hardly any of the men who were fathers of our playmates."[9]

Alexandra Kalman, practically the only one of Scott's St. Paul crowd who befriended Zelda, implied Scott's parents were part of a "tight-knit" St. Paul society because of McQuillan connections but admitted that Mollie was "'very eccentric and peculiar, and very unattractive looking,' likely to wear one blue shoe and one brown shoe and a hat twenty years out of style. 'She was a very intelligent person, a great reader, but very absentminded.'"[10] The neighborhood kids called her "Messy Mollie" as she passed them on her frequent trips to the library, "dressed rather eccentrically with hat and hair askew."[11] One of the members of Scott's dance class, Philip Stringer, agreed that Mollie was "a little weird."[12]

With such a legacy, Scott can scarcely have been considered unusual for going "around the neighborhood as a child claiming he was not the son of his parents but had been found on the Fitzgerald doorstep one cold morning wrapped in a blanket to which was pinned a paper bearing on it the regal name of 'Stuart.'"[13]

Sigmund Freud, for one, would have found Scott's reaction quite understandable. A "growing sense of dissatisfaction with his parents," Freud claimed, can lead a "child to seek relief in the idea that he must be a stepchild or an adopted child. . . . He fancies himself the child of a prominent statesman, a millionaire, an aristocratic landowner. . . ."[14] Many, if not most, adults would certainly recognize such daydreams in their own childhood fantasies, but—unlike Scott—few would create lasting memorials to these dream worlds. During the particularly hectic summer season of

1909, a cornucopia of experiences would provide Scott with several opportunities to get away from home and imagine what it might be like to be the progeny of statesmen, aristocratic landowners, or millionaires—plus give him fodder for several of his best works.

WITHIN A SHORT TIME of emancipation from his first year at St. Paul Academy, Scott and a friend, Wharton Smith, who lived nearby on Virginia Street, took advantage of the recently opened Point Douglas Road to peddle their bicycles to Hastings.[15] One of the main attractions in the town, nestled near the spot where the Mississippi meets the St. Croix River, was the old "Spiral" or "Pig Tail" bridge built in 1895. One approach looped over itself to gain enough height for the main span. The more than forty-mile bike trip along the rolling hills of the Mississippi River valley must have exhausted the two adventurers, and Scott never again logged such a marathon ride.

Fitzgerald's 1909 signature in the Lakeside Hotel register, Frontenac. (Photo by Dave Page)

A better chance to escape the confines of St. Paul came later in the summer. Scott noted in his *Ledger* that he traveled to Frontenac, Minnesota, in July 1909 for a ten-day vacation. The register for the Frontenac Inn shows that on July 27 he signed in with Mrs. Tams Bixby and her son. Mr. Bixby was president and general manager of the *St. Paul Pioneer Press,* and the Bixby family lived at 530 Holly, only a couple blocks from the Fitzgeralds' temporary residence and within two doors of the house to which the family would eventually move in the fall.

Long before the turn of the century, Frontenac had become the destination of choice for the upper crust of St. Paul society. As early as 1873, James J. Hill and his family would board a steamer for the fifty-mile run down the Mississippi to cool themselves on the shores of Lake Pepin, a wide spot in the river. Hill enjoyed the view from the porch of the hotel at Frontenac so much he commissioned a painting of the scene.[16]

View from the front porch of the Lakeside Hotel, ca. 1910. (Courtesy Goodhue County Historical Society)

Over three decades later, the resort at Frontenac continued to attract the elite of St. Paul and other cities, thus earning the reputation as the "Newport of the Northwest."[17] During that summer of 1909, the Pierce Butler family vacationed in Frontenac while their grand home took shape at 1347 Summit Avenue. Mr. Butler was a member of the University of Minnesota Board of Regents, a respected and successful railroad and corporation attorney, and in 1922 would become a United States Supreme Court justice. The Bigelows, another prominent St. Paul business family, stopped down that summer, as did the Kalmans, whose daughter Alexandra would become one of Scott's closest friends. Her grandfather, Aaron Goodrich, was a Minnesota territory supreme court justice. Scott dutifully noted in his *Ledger* the names of several of the Butler children, the Bigelows and Kalmans as his playmates while at Frontenac.

For Scott, escaping the furnace of a St. Paul summer to be with his friends certainly provided only part of his pleasure: he must have also found it quite tempting to consider himself, at least for a few days, a permanent member of these leading families. The aura of old Frontenac could only have added to this fantasy. Surrounded by the hills overlooking the Mississippi River in southeastern Minnesota, Frontenac was, and still is, a village right out of the pages of a romance novel, and the resort's mysteries and myths intrigued Scott and his playmates; at least "Intrigue" is the word Scott used in his *Ledger.*

Despite the fact several biographers credit a 1915 trip to Montana with Princeton schoolmate Charles "Sap" Donahoe as inspiration for "The Diamond as Big as the Ritz," a comparison of that short story's setting and plot with the geography and history of Frontenac would suggest Scott used anecdotes he picked up at the resort as source material for the tale, in which "Fitzgerald deepened his perception of ambition and possession of wealth in America."[18]

The driving force behind the real-life story of Frontenac was Israel Garrard, who took a steamboat west in the early 1850s to seek his fortune. Local folklore suggests that through the use of threats, force or chicanery, he and his partners managed to secure land stretching six miles along the Mississippi. By 1857, Garrard had become sole proprietor and established himself more or less as a "feudal lord," having brought with him a number of Swiss residents of Cincinnati to act as servants.[19] The newspapers dubbed him a Southern aristocrat, but he was actually the son of a Kentuckian who married into a moneyed Cincinnati family. Scott, whose own father was a border-state citizen who propelled himself into Northern society through marriage, would have found the similarity irresistible.

Garrard's efforts to create a "Minnesota Eden"[20] were interrupted by the Civil War, during which he rose to the rank of brigadier general in the Union Army. He returned to Frontenac after the conflict ended and continued "work which wasn't duplicated until the WPA [Works Progress Administration] came into existence. There was [sic] terracing and lanes cut, a race track laid

General Israel Garrard on the shore of Lake Pepin with Lakeside Hotel in the background, ca. 1900. (Courtesy Goodhue County Historical Society)

out, and colonial houses erected."[21] The yards were expansive. One even boasted a small golf course with greens made of sand.

In "The Diamond as Big as the Ritz," published in 1922, Confederate Colonel Fitz-Norman Culpepper Washington travels west at the end of the Civil War with two dozen faithful slaves from a "played-out plantation" in Virginia. According to the story, Washington discovers a mountain-sized diamond and develops around it a large estate with forests, a lake, and a golf course. To protect this Eden, he makes sure his five square miles of property is the only land in the United States not surveyed. He accomplishes this through the use of threats, force and chicanery. Ultimately, he even has a river deflected in order to secure his secret. Fitz-Norman Washington dies in 1900 and his only son, Braddock, takes over the excavation of the diamond mountain. By the time of the young hero's arrival in the story, Braddock has discontinued mining operations.

General Israel Garrard during the Civil War. (Courtesy Goodhue County Historical Society)

Lakeside Hotel ca. 1910. (Courtesy Goodhue County Historical Society)

By comparison, General Garrard refused to allow any commercial development to spoil his fiefdom. He managed this in part because he was able to convince the Chicago, Milwaukee, St. Paul and Pacific Railroad to divert its tracks two miles inland instead of running directly alongside the Mississippi River. General Garrard died in 1901 and his only son, George, was left to carry on the family quarry business, but he had stopped operations the year before Scott's trip to Frontenac.

Even the rugged setting of Fitzgerald's story can be traced to the bluffs surrounding Frontenac. Old photographs taken about the time of Scott's visit show rutted roads that would have "knocked to pieces in half an hour" an ordinary car, as Percy Washington tells the protagonist in "The Diamond as Big as the Ritz."[22] From one of the surrounding hills, Israel's brother Jeptha conducted experiments with flying machines—the one thing fictional Percy and his father fear might be used to find them. Col. Jeptha Garrard, who had raised and equipped a cavalry troop during the Civil War, experimented on his aircraft designs in a large workshop in the back of his brother's home.[23]

General Garrard's house, called St. Hubert's Lodge in honor of the patron saint of hunting, is not as opulent as the Washington residence, but close enough. The 5,500-square foot French-American Gallery-style home with eight bedrooms still provides wonderful views of Lake Pepin from its wrap-around screened verandahs and porches.

People who come to the fictional Washington estate to tutor the children or do other work are not allowed to escape lest they reveal the whereabouts of the property. In a similar way, persons who visited the general at Frontenac were seduced by his property's splendor and charm and did not want to return to the outside world. Novelist Charles King, for instance, came for a two-week stay and ended up spending a year, writing *From the Ranks* and *The Colonel's Daughter* in one of St. Hubert's bedrooms. General Ulysses Grant paid his respects, as did Joseph Jefferson the great actor.

Braddock Washington has a landscape gardener brought to the fictional estate. Alexis Jean Fournier, the renowned landscape painter, accepted Garrard's invitation to visit St. Hubert's Lodge, as did the Rev. Henry Ward Beecher, brother of author Harriet Beecher Stowe. So many guests came, in fact, that the General converted a grain warehouse, originally built in 1859, into a hotel to accommodate them.

Initially named Lakeside Hotel in 1865, it was changed to the Frontenac Inn in 1906, just three years before Scott arrived with his budding imagination. Immediately after Scott settled into the hotel, he received a telegram from his father who enclosed one dollar and admonished Scott "to spend it liberally, generously, judiciously, sensibly. Get from it pleasure, wisdon [sic], health and experience"—a job even tougher than it sounds since the only commercial establishment was the hotel. At the beginning of "The Diamond as Big as the Ritz," John T. Unger also gets a gift of

From this hill, Jeptha Garrard conducted his flying machine experiences. The Lakeside Hotel sits on the Peninsula off the bow of the steamboat, ca. 1910. (Courtesy Goodhue County Historical Society)

money from his father. The Ungers hail from a small Mississippi River town which Scott named Hades. Interestingly, that summer of 1909 the temperature in St. Paul reached 107 degrees, causing five people to die of heat stroke.

SCOTT'S SISTER, ANNABEL, had visited Frontenac on June 17 with friend Laura Fulton, but was in Duluth with her mother when Scott arrived at the Lakeside Hotel. Scott had plenty of other friends available for activities. Jean and Georgie Ingersoll (whose last name made it into such stories as the St. Paul-based "A Short Trip Home"), Josephine and Cecilia Kalman,[24] and Suzanne Rice—all acquaintances from St. Paul—had ventured down earlier in July.

Scott, however, focused his attentions on Evelyn Stuart Garrard, the daughter of George Garrard and his wife Virginia. Known for his notorious spelling, Fitzgerald first scrawled what appears to be "Evylyn Garard"[25] in his *Ledger*, then changed the spelling to "Girard." Unlike the one brother and one sister Kismine had in "The Diamond as Big as the Ritz," Evelyn had two sisters. Like the siblings in the story, however, the Garrard daughters lived at their father's gingerbread mansion (Winona Cottage, the home General Garrard built for his son directly above Frontenac Inn) but traveled extensively. Kismine's sister Jasmine, for example, plans to come out in London; Beulah, Evelyn's sister, eventually made her home in England's capital.

Evelyn was able to steer her new friends to such curiosities as the site of Fort Beauharnois, built by the French in 1727 on land now occupied by Villa Marie, and In-Yan-Teopa, a rock opening where Indians worshiped and the possible inspiration for Fitzgerald's reference to "The Cave at Frontenac" in his *Ledger*. As readers will recall, Braddock Washington, his wife, his son and their remaining slaves disappear into a "trap-door in the side of the [diamond] mountain" near the end of "The Diamond as Big as the Ritz."[26] For the most part, however, these places did not hold the gang's attention for long. Evelyn's son, Garrard Beck, who spent summers at Winona Cottage playing with the younger hotel guests,

In-Yan-Teopa, possibly, the "Cave at Frontenac," ca. 1910. (Courtesy Goodhue County Historical Society)

did not remember his mother ever mentioning Fitzgerald. He did recall the local sites as being "as suspect as Santa Claus and about as interesting. In-Yan-Teopa . . . was a one-time shot, rather like Grant's tomb."[27]

For Fitzgerald, however, Frontenac was not a "one-time shot." Fitzgerald returned the summer before entering Princeton in 1913. "Visiting the Girards," he noted in his *Ledger.* "I love her—oh—oh—oh."[28] Although he managed once more to misspell the name of his infatuation, his 16-year-old passion is clear, just as John Unger's for Kismine is evident in the pages of Fitzgerald's story.

Over a decade after he wrote the story, Scott listed "Frontenac" in his notebook under the heading "Nostalgia or the Flight of the Heart." His title for the section in *Tales of the Jazz Age* that included "The Diamond as Big as The Ritz" was "Fantasies." As Scott said in his table of contents to *Tales of the Jazz Age,* the story developed from "that familiar mood characterized by a perfect craving for luxury,"[29] a desire he certainly developed as a youngster. Yet in all respects, "The Diamond as Big as the Ritz" tells readers that great wealth can just as easily trap as it can provide luxuries. The story thus serves to show the conflict between the American dream, and the American reality. In that sense, "The Diamond as Big as the Ritz" certainly foreshadows other Fitzgerald stories such as "The Swimmer." According to Robert Emmet Long, the story also "anticipates *The Great Gatsby* in its concern with the national ideal of wealth . . . and in its focusing of national aspiration through the American West."[30]

But these ruminations took place several years and a few score miles away when Scott was living in another Minnesota resort community on a different lake in 1922. In the summer of 1909, returning to St. Paul on August 7 must have been difficult for

Scott. Not only would he have to leave Evelyn, but Jim Porterfield, a St. Paul friend, had reached Frontenac only the day before, and one of Scott's favorites, Alida Bigelow, arrived the day he left.

Whatever role Scott managed to carve for himself in the genteel resort, he must have shared the feelings of his creation John Unger, who—as summer drew to a close—"began to regret that he must soon go back to school."[31] Yet Scott's fantasies did not have to evaporate after he left Frontenac. He could continue to dream of vast riches as he headed north to join his sister and mother in Duluth, the prosperous Great Lakes port from which the three would board a passenger boat for a visit to Buffalo, New York.

Duluth Harbor, ca 1909. (Courtesy Duluth Public Library)

As the wealth of the Northwest poured through Duluth's harbor for transit east, some of it slipped off trains and ore boats and remained behind. Newspaper articles in the Duluth dailies during the summer of 1909 featured photographs of new buildings: a larger high school, an ornate train station, and Glensheen, a baronial manor fronting Lake Superior just north of the city.

But for the future creator of Jay Gatsby, the image which burned its way more than any other onto Scott's impressionable mind was Thomas F. Cole's yacht *Alvina*, riding at anchor in Duluth harbor. The 214-foot pleasure vessel sailed amidst much fanfare into Duluth harbor just a few weeks before Scott's arrival.[32] Cole, his son, and friends had cruised from Cleveland, where the *Alvina* had been refitted at U.S. Steel's shipbuilding facilities.

Close-up of the *Alvina*, ca. 1909. (Courtesy Duluth Marine Museum)

Tom Cole. (Courtesy of the Northeast Minnesota Historical Center)

As president of Oliver Mining Company, a subsidiary of U.S. Steel, Cole was the acme of glamour and may have provided Fitzgerald with part of the model for Dan Cody, Jay Gatsby's mentor in *The Great Gatsby*. Fitzgerald himself credits Robert Kerr—a Great Neck, New York, acquaintance—for the creation of Cody.[33] Kerr told Scott a story about rowing out to a yacht to warn the owner of a dangerous tide.[34] (A watchful editor kept Scott from mistakenly putting a tide in Lake Superior.) While Cody may have started his literary life as a neighbor's tale, he wound up in *The Great Gatsby* as an extension of Fitzgerald's own experience: the similarities between Cody and Cole are just too numerous to be coincidental.[35]

Like Cody, Cole made his money from copper interests in Montana; and like Jay Gatz, Scott must have fantasized as he sat by Duluth harbor that Cody would pick him up and take him for a cruise on the gleaming white *Alvina*. After all, this was the same young boy who—when he was four years old—"wore a blue sailor suit & told enormous lies to older people about being really the owner of a real yatch [sic]."[36]

Coincidentally, several writers have noted that Scott began planning *Gatsby*, his third novel, while at the White Bear Yacht Club in Dellwood, just a few miles north of hometown St. Paul. In a letter to Max Perkins penned at the club sometime in June 1922, Scott indicated his intention to "write something new—something extraordinary and beautiful and simple and intricately patterned." Later he expanded the concept by suggesting its "locale will be the Middle West and New York of 1885. . . . It will have a Catholic element."[37] Much of the Catholic element—which included the background of Jay Gatz—was cut from the novel and ended up as the story "Absolution." A much abbreviated version of Gatsby's young adulthood was spliced into *Gatsby*, including the Kerr episode—after it had been filtered through Fitzgerald's own experience in Duluth. This is how Scott described seeing the yacht in *The Great Gatsby*:

To young Gatz, resting on his oars and looking up at the railed deck, that yacht represented all the beauty and glamor in the world. I suppose he smiled at Cody—he had probably discovered that people liked him when he smiled. At any rate Cody asked him a few questions (one of them elicited the brand new name) and found that he was quick and extravagantly ambitious. A few days later he took him to Duluth and bought him a blue coat, six pairs of white duck trousers, and a yachting cap. And when the *Tuolomee* left for the West Indies and the Barbary Coast Gatsby left too.[38]

Cody's yacht in *The Great Gatsby* even bears a name similar to one of Cole's mining interests, the Tuolumne Copper Company of Butte, Montana.[39] Admittedly, this is a remarkable account to draw from the well of memory while a dozen years and a continent away, but there is quite a bit of circumstantial evidence pointing to a link between Cole and Cody, besides the remarkable similarity of their names. The man who lived across the street from the Fitzgeralds in 1909 and to whose house they themselves would move in September 1910, Stuart Shotwell, was "a promoter and heavy owner of the Tuolumne mines in Montana."[40] Scott witnessed the death of Mr. Shotwell in May 1910 when the latter was struck by a car. "Young Scott Fitzgerald" was quoted in the newspaper the following day, so he at the very least read about Shotwell's connection to the Tuolumne Copper Company at that point if he had not heard of it before. From Shotwell there may have been a link to Cole, whose biography seems to have been used by Fitzgerald for his description of Dan Cody in *The Great Gatsby.*

> Cody was fifty years old then [Cole was forty-seven when Scott was in Duluth], a product of the Nevada silver fields [Cole owned mining interests in that state]. . . . transactions in Montana copper . . . made him many times a millionaire. [Cole was president of North Butte, Montana, Copper Company, which became famous for its bonanza copper ore.][41]

Cody had, as recorded in *Gatsby*, been drifting around Lake Superior and turned up as James Gatz's destiny in Little Girl Bay. Similarly, Cole delighted in taking the *Alvina* on trips out of its home port into Lake Superior, and he may have passed Little Girl's Point on Lake Superior's South Shore about fifty miles east of Ashland, Wisconsin. These excursions were duly reported in the Duluth News.

To any young man hoping to make an impression on the world, Cole could easily have served as a mentor. His was a real-life rags to riches story. Three years prior to Scott's visit to Duluth, everyone on Wall Street was asking "Who's Cole?"[42] This former mine worker and railroad breakman shunned publicity, concentrating his efforts instead on working his way up the iron ore hierarchy, finally earning a spot in the Steel Trust as vice president of Oliver Mining. Within a year he was its president, and in less than

Venetian Night, ca 1910.
(Courtesy Northeast
Minnesota Historical Center.
Hugh McKenzie photo)

a decade, this six-footer was able to pay $25 million for control of all Montana copper mines outside of Amalgamated Copper Company.

But Scott was not as fortunate as Kerr, who, like Gatsby, had been hired by the yachtsman he had warned. Scott's only chance to approach Cole and his yacht probably occurred during Venetian Night—a large social gathering sponsored by the Duluth Boat Club on the evening of August 9, the day after Scott met his mother in Duluth. The boat club began this reenactment of the ancient festival of Venice two years earlier at its new home on Park Point, the longest fresh water sand bar in the world. Unlike the rest of the Duluth area, the natural stand of pine on the bar had not been logged off, and these conifers provided a cool backdrop for the club's activities.[43] On Venetian Night, six to seven thousand spectators stood in awe as 140 canoes, rowboats, and sailboats ablaze with Japanese lanterns paraded along the water.[44]

Those Christmas tree-like ships bobbing in Duluth harbor were quite dazzling; however, all eyes were riveted on the center of the harbor as the "elaborately decorated boats were led out into the bay and around Thomas F. Cole's yacht, the *Alvina*. . . . brightly lighted from stem to stern for the occasion, they not faintly reproduced in the mind the pictures and descriptions of the luxuriously equipped craft with which the beautiful Cleopatra was wont to travel the Nile."[45] It is hard to imagine that this image of Cole's yacht floating majestically in a blazing sea of luminous butterflies, dragons and other creatures did not leave a permanent image in Scott's mind; but if Fitzgerald had any direct contact with Cole, it has not been recorded. Henry Dan Piper noted, however, that "knowing of Fitzgerald's interest.in 'success' stories" of Midwesterners making millions and coming out East, his Long Island friends collected newspaper accounts of such people.[46] Since Cole appeared in the New York papers, it is possible that Scott may have learned or relearned about him through clippings.

Whether or not Scott developed an interest in Montana copper during his stay with "Sap" Donahoe, he certainly seemed fascinated by the state and its ore. In "The Rich Boy," published shortly after Gatsby and likewise set in the environs of New York City, Fitzgerald mentions an estate on Long Island belonging "to a cousin of Anson's who had married a Montana copper operator."[47]

The only mention Scott made of Duluth in his *Ledger* was a reference to appendicitis.[48] This was not the first nor last time Scott cried "wolf" with the intestinal inflamation. In fact, appendicitis seemed to be Fitzgerald's disease of choice. In January of the same year as his Duluth trip—along with swimming, boxing and taking showers at the YMCA—Scott recorded in his *Ledger* an earlier "Appendicitis attack."[49] Amory's "appendix burst" in *This Side of Paradise*,[50] and appendicitis manages to work its way into *The Great Gatsby*. During the party at Myrtle and Tom's apartment in New York City, Myrtle says to her sister that "I had a woman up here last week to look at my feet and when she gave me the bill you'd of thought she had my appendicitus [sic] out."[51] The year after *The Great Gatsby* was published, while traveling with Zelda to Hollywood (Scott had been hired to work for United Artists as a script writer), Zelda recalled in a letter to daughter Scottie:

> Daddy got so nervous [on the train trip West] he thought he had an appendicitis so we had to get out and spend the night at a place called El Paso on the Mexican border—but he was well by the time we got to the hotel.[52]

Scott recovered in Duluth as well, and he, his mother and sister continued their journey to Buffalo.

The Anchor Line was one of the few steamship companies with direct trips to Buffalo from Duluth, and the threesome boarded one of its two available ships for the trip across the Great Lakes. Named after rivers in Pennsylvania, the ships had green hulls and gleaming white cabins reminiscent of Cole's yacht. At a top speed of fifteen knots, the voyage took three to four days, the passengers sleeping in cabins on board.[53] To Scott and his fertile imagination, the Anchor Line ship became the *Alvina*; his short

The Anchor Line steamer *Tionesta,* ca. 1910. F. Scott Fitzgerald sailed to Buffalo in 1909 on a ship such as this. (Courtesy Duluth Marine Museum)

pants, white ducks; and his trip "Abroad," the word he used in his *Ledger,* a world cruise with Tom Cole.

Notes

1 *F. Scott Fitzgerald's Ledger: A Facsimile* (Washington, D.C.: A Bruccoli Clark Book, 1972), 163. In the introduction, Matthew Bruccoli writes: "It is impossible to be certain when Fitzgerarld began keeping the *Ledger,* bit 1919/1920—at the start of his career—seems likely...."

2 Andrew Turnbull, *The Letters of F. Scott Fitzgerald* (New York: Dell Publishing Co., Inc., 1966), 221-222.

3 *Ibid., 563.*

4 John Kuehl, ed., *The Apprentice Fiction of F. Scott Fitzgerald* (New Brunswick, N.J.: Rutgers University Press, 1965), 178.

5 F. Scott Fitzgerald, *Tender is the Night* (New York: Charles Scribner's Sons, 1962), 203.

6 Tony Buttitta, *The Lost Summer: A Personal Memoir of F. Scott Fizgerald* (New York: St. Martin's Press, 1987), 41.

7 Margot Kriel, "Fitzgerald in St. Paul: People Who Knew Him Reminisce," in *University of Minnesota Conference on F. Scott Fizgerald, Conference Proceedings,* 29-31 October 1982, 23

8 *Ibid.,* 24.

9 *Ibid.,* 24.

10 *Ibid.,* 24.

11 Beth Kent, "Fitzgerald's Back in Town," *The Grand Gazette,* August 1973, 7.

12 Philip Stringer. Interview with authors. St. Paul, Minnesota, 1 March 1984.

13 Henry Dan Piper, "The Untrimmed Christmas Tree: The Religious Background of *The Great Gatsby,*" in Henry Dan Piper, ed., *Fitzgerald's The Great Gatsby: The Novel, The Critics, The Background* (New York: Charles Scribner's Sons, 1970), 96. Given Scott's fascination with the Civil War, however, listeners might easily assume "Stuart" referred to

J.E.B. Stuart, the Confederate cavalry commander.

14 Maria Tatar, *The Hard Facts of the Grimms' Fairy Tales* (Princeton, N.J.: Princeton University Press, 1987), 74.

15 *Ledger,* 163.

16 Phil Duff, "James Hill: 'Robber barron [sic],'" *Red Wing Republican Eagle,* 13 June 1983, 5.

17 Ivan Kubista, *This Quiet Dust: A Chronicle of Old Frontenac* (Old Frontenac: Old Frontenac Heritage Preservation Commission, 1978),

18 Robert Sklar, *F. Scott Fizgerald: The Last Laocoön* (New York: Oxford University Press, 1967), 147.

19 Jack Keefe, "Pastoral Charm of Old Frontenac Periled by Will of the Late Owner," *Minneapolis Tribune,* 10 September 1938, 5.

20 Kubista, *Quite Dust,* 57.

21 Keefe, "Old Frontenac," 5.

22 Matthew Bruccoli, ed., *The Short Stories of F. Scott Fitzgerald* (New York: Charles Scribner's Sons, 1989), 187.

23 Sara Schouweiler, "Minnesotan's Plane Failed," *St. Paul Pioneer Press,* 7 December 1947, 4.

24 A few years after the General's death, St. Hubert's became the summer home of St. Paul resident Rukard Hurd, who wrote his "Iron Ore Manual" there. Mr. and Mrs. Hurd often played host to the Kalman sisters, including Cecilia, good friends of Scott's.

25 *Ledger,* 163; Frances Densmore, "The Garrard Family in Frontenac," *Minnesota History,* March 1933, 43.

26 Malcolm Cowley, ed., *The Stories of F. Scott Fitzgerald* (New York: Charles Scribner's Sons, 1951), 36.

27 Garrard Beck. Letter to authors, 16 December 1983.

28 *Ledger,* 167.

29 F. Scott Fitzgerald, *Tales of the Jazz Age* (New York: Charles Scribner's Sons, 1922), viii.

30 Robert Long, *The Achieving of The Great Gatsby: F. Scott Fitzgerald, 1920-1925* (London: Bucknell University Press, 1979), 67.

31 Bruccoli, *Short Stories,* 203.

32 "The 'Alvina,' Beautiful New Pleasure Yacht Purchased by Thomas F. Cole," *Duluth Evening Herald,* 3 July 1909, 6; "T.F. Cole's Yacht Due," *Duluth News Tribune,* 14 July 1909, 10.

33 The actual name Dan Cody, although remarkably similar to Cole, probably came from one of Zelda's beaus by the same name, just as the name of Daisy's friend in *The Great Gatsby* may have come from one of Zelda's circle of friends: Jordan Prince. Sara Mayfield, *Exiles from Paradise* (New York: Dell Publishing Company, Inc., 1974), 46.

34 James Mellow, *Invented Lives: F. Scott and Zelda Fitzgerald* (Boston: Houghton Mifflin, 1984), 194; Bruccoli, *Correspondence,* 143.

35 There are, however, some interesting coincidences arising from the Oliver Mining Company connection. Three decades after Scott left

Duluth, the company would pass into the hands of Leroy Salsich, husband of novelist Margaret Culkin Banning. Oliver Mining would eventually bid on the Major Stars semi-pro baseball club, which included many of the team members from the infamous 1919 Chicago White Sox team that threw the World Series. The scandal played a minor role in *The Great Gatsby* and probably worked its way into the novel because of another Great Neck neighbor and a drinking partner of Scott's, Ring Lardner, who was a baseball fan and deeply hurt by the affair. Pete Dexter, "Black Sox Blues," *Esquire,* October 1984, 265.

36 *Ledger,* 155.

37 Piper, "The Untrimmed Christmas Tree," 93.

38 F. Scott Fitzgerald, *The Great Gatsby* (New York: Scribner Paperback Fiction, 1995), 106.

39 The company name may have come from a central California Indian Tribe. Today, there is a Tuolumne County in northern California, and the Tuolumne River is San Francisco's chief source of water. Cole committed suicide in his Pasadena, California, home in 1939. Since the river is pronounced Twal-oo-me, Fitzgerald may have simply misspelled it. Interestingly, the single word "Tuolmans" appears in Scott's notebook, which he compiled from several different sources sometime after 1932. Matthew Bruccoli, ed., *The Notebooks of F. Scott Fitzgerald.* New York: Harcourt Brace Jovanovich, 1978), 146. John Callahan in *The Illusions of a Nation: Myth and History in the Novels of F. Scott Fitzgerald* (Urbana: University of Illinois Press, 1972), 50, suggests the name Tuolomee came from a river in the Alaskan gold fields.

40 "Girl Autoist Kills Broker," *St. Paul Pioneer Press,* 23 May 1910, 2.

41 Fitzgerald, *Gatsby,* 105.

42 "Cole Hidden Power in Great Mine Deals," *The New York Times,* 18 February 1906, 7.

43 Michael Cochran, "A Historical Study of the Duluth Boat Club, 1896-1926," M.A. Diss., University of Minnesota.

44 "Boat Club Hot Weather Solace," *Duluth News Tribune,* 5 August 1909, 4; "Thousands Enjoy Water Spectacle," *Duluth News Tribune,* 10 August 1909, 4.

45 "Thousands."

46 Henry Dan Piper, "The Fuller-McGee Case," in Henry Dan Piper, ed., *Fitzgerald's The Great Gatsby* (New York: Charles Scribner's Sons, 1970), 171.

47 F. Scott Fitzgerald, *Babylon Revisited and Other Stories* (New York: Charles Scribner's Sons, 1971), 170.

48 If Scott had indeed suffered from appendicitis, he would have been in good hands. Dr. W.H. McGee had been performing appendectomies in Duluth for some time prior to 1909. According to Dr. Mike Zlonis, McGee had operated on John D. Rockefeller, Jr., when he was stricken with appendicitis in Duluth in 1905. McGee makes no mention of the Fitzgeralds in his log for the month of August 1909. Mike Zlonis, M.D. Telephone conversation with authors, 18 February 1984.

49 *Ledger,* 163.

50 Fitzgerald, *Paradise,* 7.

51 Fitzgerald, *Gatsby,* 35.

52 Nancy Milford, *Zelda* (New York: Harper & Row, 1970), 127.

53 Pat Labadie. Letters to authors, 1 May 1984; 3 May 1984.

Chapter Four

Published Author
1909 to 1911

I want to be one of the greatest writers that ever lived, don't you?

Attributed to F. Scott Fitzgerald
by Edmond Wilson in,
"Thoughts on being
Bibliographed," *Princeton
University Library Chronicle*

Back in St. Paul for the start of another school year. Scott Fitzgerald and his family moved out of Grandmother McQuillan's apartment at Laurel Terrace into a duplex at 514 Holly. Although still far from what could be called financially independent, Edward had finally managed to bring together the family under its own roof.

Fitzgerald began his second year at St. Paul Academy with a flurry of activity, hiking with the boy scouts, attending University of Minnesota football games, and taking an interest in coins (perhaps due to the release of the Lincoln penny that year). Anxiously awaiting the arrival of his first published story in the October issue of the school magazine *Now and Then*, he tried unsuccessfully to garner a copy from the printers before it was finished. Frustrated in his attempt, he had to wait. "Nothing interested me until Monday," he recalled, "and when at recess, a big pile of the copies were brought in and delivered to the business manager I was so excited that I bounced in my seat and mumbled to myself, 'They're here! They're here!' until the whole school looked at me in amazement."[1]

His first published story, "The Mystery of the Raymond Mortgage," remains somewhat of a mystery because the young writer never explains who stole the mortgage or why. Obviously influenced by Sir Arthur Conan Doyle (one of the key characters even utilizes street children to do his bidding as did the immortal

Fitzgerald House, 514 Holly.
(Photo by Dave Page)

Sherlock Holmes), the story centers around a double murder, an unlikely pursuit, and a confession. This overly melodramatic, undistinguished start to a literary legend's career best serves as a reminder to aspiring artists that everyone has to begin somewhere.

Even more important to Fitzgerald than his literary accomplishments were his forays into athletics. He again tried his hand at football and actually made the academy team as a substitute. He did see limited action in a single game. The opponents were of such inferior size that the coach decided to prevent a massacre by utilizing his own lighter men. Nothing of importance followed; there were no romps to glory.[2] In later gridiron contests he proved he had guts by expressing a desire to play despite a broken rib and other injuries, but determination alone was not enough for Fitzgerald to gain renown for handling the pigskin. One of his contemporaries remembered him as being "certainly no athlete."[3]

In response to his failure, Fitzgerald philosophized "that if you weren't able to function in action you might at least be able to tell about it, because you felt the same intensity—it was a back door way out of facing reality."[4] His second published story in *Now and Then* (February 1910) provided a balm of sorts for mediocrity on the field. In "Reade, Substitute Right Half," the central figure is "a light haired stripling," quite naturally a mirror of Fitzgerald. Unlike his creator, however, Reade manages to become a hero by scoring a touchdown.

Encouraged by fellow students and faculty, the budding author followed his first successes with a pair of Civil War-related stories, "A Debt of Honor" and "The Room with the Green Blinds." His return to writing with a historical bent was quite understandable given his interest in history and the Civil War. Still, he was by no means giving up on sports. After football season, Fitzgerald turned his attention to basketball and baseball. On the basketball court he saw little or no action despite being on the third team; he did just as poorly on the baseball squad, earning the spot of second string pitcher on the third team.

In retrospect, the highlight of the school year was his enrollment in classes at Ramaley School of Dance. Located at 664-668 Grand, one block south of Summit, the pink-and-white ballroom opened in 1902 upstairs of F.W. Ramaley's catering service, delicatessen, and bakery. Jean Ingersoll's mother, Mrs. Janey MacLaren Ingersoll, organized the classes by contacting other families in the neighborhood and announcing the formation of a class.[5] Mollie was one of the parents who responded to Mrs. Ingersoll's invitation, and her son, who had earlier attended dance classes with Mr. Van Arnem in Buffalo, became one of the pupils.

Although the Edward Fitzgeralds were not as financially independent as many of the other students' families, F. Scott was accepted by his classmates because "Janey Ingersoll liked him; he was a nice boy, and very good looking, and everyone liked him."[6]

The dancing master was Professor William H. Baker, an apple-shaped little man with a bald dome and a gray-white mustache who moonlighted as a bartender at the White Bear Yacht

Professor Baker's dancing class. Ramaley Hall, April 1910. First Row: McNeil Seymour, Leonard Shepley, Betty Hester, Archie Jackson, Hamilton Hersey, Betty Mudge, Eleanor Mitchell, Cecil Read, Henry Adams, and Truman Gardner. Second Row: Dorothy Greene, Kitty Schulze, Margaret Horn, Egbert Driscoll, Elizabeth Field, Marie Hersey, Alida Bigelow, Helen James, Margaret Armstrong, Julia Door, Joanne Orton, and Professor Baker. Third Row: Donald Driscoll, Jim Porterfield, Arthur Foley, Larry Boardman, Georgie Ingersoll, Suzanne Rice, Caroline Clark, Donald Bigelow, Robert Clark, Dorothy Anderson, Jean Ingersoll, and Gus Schurmeier. Fourth Row: Ted Townsend, Jack Mitchell, Mildred Bishop, Priscilla Adams, Wharton Smith, Theodore Ames, Elisabeth Devin, Kitty Ordway, Philip Stringer, Lovell May, and F. Scott Fitzgerald. (Courtesy of the Minnesota Historical Society)

Club. For most of the students his second life was no secret since his breath often imparted just the slightest trace of alcoholic spirits.[7] Professor Baker's pupils remembered him as "an enormously fat man, but light on his feet" or "a dumpy little round man with traces of white hair," but all were in agreement that he knew his business.[8]

Classes were conducted on Saturday afternoons, each class averaging forty pupils evenly divided between the sexes. All the children lived in the neighborhood and were labeled, whether warranted or unwarranted, "The Grand Avenue Gentry," since most of them came from wealthy backgrounds. For the average male student, dancing instruction was anything but popular. Philip Stringer, one of the reluctant neophytes in Fitzgerald's class, shared his feelings: "The dancing lessons lasted all of Saturday afternoons and completely ruined our Saturdays. After going to school all week, the only day we had to ourselves was Saturday, and it had to be wasted learning the Grand March."[9]

Although the boys generally despised the lessons, most of the girls enjoyed the Saturday sessions. Here was an opportunity to meet with friends away from the classroom, learn some new dances, and size up the neighborhood's eligible squires. The young ladies took great pride in learning the steps and gigglish delight in knowing that the boys were uncomfortable. They smiled at one another over the conduct of the male pupils, who were often involved in antics which led to scolding.[10]

The girls would arrive at Ramaley's wearing their party dresses and carrying slippers, eager participants in a fashion show.[11] The boys, too, at least dressed the part. Stringer remembered them wearing "serge suits of blue cloth, knickers, Windsor ties, black patent leather shoes, white cotton gloves, and starched collars of the variety worn at Eton glamour school in England."[12]

Although Jean Ingersoll and Betty Jackson, whose brother Ted Ames was in Fitzgerald's dance class, both rated Scott as an excellent dancer,[13] at least one of his partners at Ramaley's remembered quite the opposite: "He . . . had no sense of rhythm . . . besides being physically awkward. But he loved dancing class . . ."[14] Whatever his skill level, Scott's enthusiasm made him a favorite of Professor Baker, and he eventually put the lessons to good use. Perhaps his most important dancing feat was his success at sweeping his future wife Zelda off her feet: "There seemed to be some heavenly support beneath his shoulder blades. . . ," she remembered about their dancing, "as if he secretly enjoyed the ability to fly but was walking as a compromise to convention."[15] In her autobiographical novel, *Save Me the Waltz,* Zelda describes her heroine's attraction to the character based on Scott: "Dancing with [him], he smelled like new goods. Being close to him with her face in the space between his ear and his stiff army collar was like being initiated into the subterranean reserves of a fine fabric store. . . ."[16]

Dances and dancing provide a backdrop for scenes in many of Scott's stories and novels as well. "I gave her up to the bright restless sea of the dance," Fitzgerald wrote in "A Short Trip

Home," "where she moved in an eddy of her own among the pleasant islands of colored favors set out on tables and the south winds from the brasses moaning across the hall."[17] In "Winter Dreams," Dexter Green is watching the dancers at the University Club when Judy Jones approaches him: "A breeze of warmth and light blew through the room," Fitzgerald says of her effect on Dexter.[18] And, of course, Marjorie in "Bernice Bobs Her Hair" claims other women would give ten years of their lives to have three or four men in love with them and "be cut in on every few feet at dances.[19]

This list of stories with references to dancing goes on and on. Yet, it is in *The Great Gatsby* where Fitzgerald perhaps puts to best use his time at Ramaley Hall. For starters, the Ordways, Herseys and Schulzes he mentions at the end of the novel were members of his dancing class. Much more significant, however, are the references to posture and poise, important elements of dance. Early in the novel, for example, Nick Carraway pays Gatsby a compliment by saying that he is "gorgeous" because of his "unbroken series of successful gestures."[20] Similarly, Daisy finds offensive the seduction of a starlet at one of Gatsby's parties "because it wasn't a gesture but an emotion."[21] Although Daisy, Tom and Jordan have had years of practicing poses and gestures, the things one learns at dance lessons when the instructor reminds his or her students to keep their backs straight and their necks stretched, Gatsby is relatively new at the charade. His calling of acquaintances "Old Sport" marks him as a poseur; whereas Jordan "with her chin raised a little as if she were balancing something on it which was quite likely to fall,"[22] is a true member of the leisure class. She maintains an "erect carriage . . . by throwing her body backward at the shoulders like a young cadet"[23]; and during the fight between Tom and Jay in the Plaza Hotel, Jordan again begins "to balance an invisible but absorbing object on the tip of her chin," while at the same time Gatsby appears "as if he had 'killed a man.'"[24] Even at the end of her relationship with Nick, she steadfastly keeps "her chin raised a little, jauntily."[25]

Ultimately, it is Daisy and Tom who provide readers with the most subtle lesson about partners. Although Jay can manage a "graceful and conservative fox trot,"[26] it is Daisy and Tom who refuse to give up their collective space by caving in for other dancers. They hold their frame at all costs, even if it means they occasionally "smashed up things and creatures," as Fitzgerald put it at the end of *The Great Gatsby*, for they can retreat "back into their money or their vast carelessness, or whatever it was that kept them together, and let other people clean up the mess they had made. . . ."[27] Even if Nick suggests he cannot fathom what keeps Tom and Daisy together, Fitzgerald no doubt understood the nature of the class system in the United States. Among other things, dance lessons were reserved for the leisure class, the class to which Jay Gatz aspires. It is into this practically impenetrable upper crust of society, for which the sacrosanct space of the dancing couple provides a good metaphor, that Jay Gatsby tries to force himself.

"I feel far away from her," he tells Nick. "It's hard to make her understand."

"You mean about the dance?" Nick asks.

"The dance?" Jay responds, unsure what Nick means. Then he dismisses "all the dances he had given with a snap of his fingers. 'Old sport, the dance is unimportant.'"[28]

That is Jay's mistake. Elements distinguishing one social stratum from another, such as dancing lessons, are not unimportant. Fitzgerald himself had previewed such an opinion in his first two novels. In the "Code of the Young Egotist" section of *This Side of Paradise*, the protagonist lists being "a supple dancer" as one of the attributes that marks him as an aristocrat.[29] In *The Beautiful and Damned*, Maury, a philosophical friend of the damned Anthony, asks "What is a gentleman anyway?" After several comic responses, Muriel offers: "A man who comes from a good family and went to Yale or Harvard or Princeton, and has money and dances well, and all that."

"At last," Maury quips, "the perfect definition! Cardinal Newman's is now a back number."[30]

No doubt Maury is being sarcastic, but Muriel is speaking for Fitzgerald here. In the world of "good" families, prestigious schools, and skilled dancing, Gatsby is doomed to fail—his goal "already behind him," as Fitzgerald writes on the last page of the novel—not because of who he had become, but because of who he had been, a "Mr. Nobody from Nowhere," as Tom calls him.[31] "In [this] quintessentially male drama of poor boys becoming rich boys," one critic writes of *The Great Gatsby*, ". . . the rich boy, fearing finally for his territory, repossesses the girl and, by asking "Who is he," strips the poor boy of his presumed power. . . ."[32]

SOME BIOGRAPHERS HAVE OVERLY emphasized the conflicts Scott had while attending St. Paul Academy. The fact is that he possessed many loyal friends in the neighborhood. Benjamin Griggs remembered Scott as "vivacious, interested in people, a leader, a center of conversation. He had a very bright mind."[33] More than one friend told an interviewer in the 1970s that he had "beautiful manners," a trait not overlooked by their mothers and fathers: "Our parents were always pointing him out as an example to us kids. But we really didn't resent it."[34] Jean Ingersoll agreed. Scott was "very attractive, bright, likable. . . ," she said. "He was . . . good company. . . ."[35]

A major activity arena for Scott and this group of close friends during those long winter months was Jean's backyard at 404 Ashland. Many of the gang spent their free time here, among them Donald and Alida Bigelow, Bob and Carrie Clark, Donald and Egbert Driscoll, Cecil Read, Philip Stringer, Arthur Foley, and Fitzgerald. Jean's father, George, was responsible for attracting a good portion of the neighborhood children because he had constructed a gigantic homemade toboggan slide. On cold winter nights, he would climb the slide and pour buckets of water down the runway to improve the speed of the run, and the next day, the children would gather once again, often coasting all the way to the far side of Western Avenue.[36]

Sleigh riding, or bob parties as they were called, was another activity Fitzgerald and his friends enjoyed during the frigid months. Horses and sleighs were rented at the livery stable on Selby and Western. No matter how much the children wore, the brisk Minnesota winds penetrated them to the bone.[37] Nevertheless, bob parties were romantic affairs—the colder the better! The stars, the clumping of the horses' hooves on the brick pavements, the exchange of stories, jokes, and laughter—all contributed to an adventure Fitzgerald would capture years later in his short stories. Snuggling to keep warm, the children would ride down Summit Avenue with only the gaslit street corners, lights from the Victorian windows, and the moon for illumination.

If it was too cold to remain on the sleigh, the riders would take turns jumping off and running alongside to revive slowed circulation. Often this exercise provided an excuse for a young man to run behind with his favorite, but the chaperones made sure that no one lagged too far behind.[38] "Nowhere but Minnesota," Fitzgerald remembered, "had they such sleigh rides."[39]

Frequently the destination of the outing would be the Town and Country Club. There the children would descend and rush inside the clubhouse to sip hot chocolate.[40] Out on the verandah, the scenic cliffs of the Mississippi River huddled at their feet and Minneapolis twinkled in the distance.

Moved by these icy escapades, Fitzgerald captured their essence in *This Side of Paradise*:

> Overhead the sky was half crystalline, half misty and the night around was chill and vibrant with rich tension. From the Country Club steps the road stretched away, dark creases on the white blanket; huge heaps of snow lining the sides like the tracks of giant moles. They lingered for a moment on the steps, and watched the white holiday moon.[41]

The Town & Country Club, ca. 1900. (Courtesy of the Town & Country Club)

As the snow began to melt in April, Fitzgerald and other students in the dance class looked forward to the annual cotillion or german that concluded the five-month struggle of wills. Many of the students were of the opinion this adjournment party was the only nice thing about dance class.[42] Each pupil would dress in a silly costume, and Professor Baker would present a prize to the student who had made the greatest improvement during the course. The boys handed favors to the girls, and occasionally the girls gave little presents to the boys.

With dancing class terminated, Fitzgerald had his Saturdays back. Sometimes Scott and his companions would attend the theater as a group. Following the matinee, they would converge upon George J. Smith's candy store, which was conveniently located next to the Orpheum. Here the youngsters would linger to discuss the film and current gossip. Installed at every table in the store was a telephone to convey ice cream and candy orders, and each member in the group wanted to be the one to send the order to the front.[43] The candy store made it several times into the pages of Fitzgerald's fiction. In "He Thinks He's Wonderful," for example, Joe Gorman says "we'll all go to Smith's for ice-cream soda."[44]

The coming of nicer weather also meant professional baseball, and, like many others from St. Paul, Scott Fitzgerald went to cheer on the hometown Saints. The ball park at Lexington and University avenues was built in 1897 by Charles Comiskey. He spared no expense, even including backs on the bleacher seats. Around the turn of the century, the American Association was formed with St. Paul as a member of the league that included teams from cross-river rival Minneapolis, Toledo, Indianapolis, Louisville, Columbus, and Kansas City. But on May 22, 1910, with young Scott Fitzgerald in attendance, the Saints were hosting Milwaukee. The Brewers won both games of the double header, pushing the Saints out of first place in the standings and allowing the Millers from Minneapolis to edge ahead. The St. Paul fans were not too happy and went after the umpire. They began throwing "seat cushions, pop bottles and other debris. . . ."[45] The catcher from the Brewers went to aid the umpire and was knocked unconscious by a bottle.

The rowdy crowd of 12,000 eventually filed out of the packed stadium. Some of them began walking down Lexington around 7:00 P.M. when Stuart Shotwell, who lived across the street from the Fitzgeralds, was hit and killed by a car driven by Theodora Stark, an eighteen-year-old Minneapolis woman. She was arrested and spent the night in the St. Paul jail. The next morning, the mayor of Minneapolis came to take her home.

Although most of the witnesses indicated that Miss Stark was traveling at a low rate of speed, "Young Scott Fitzgerald" disagreed: "Mr. Shotwell started to cross the street. I saw the automobile coming; there was a woman driving and two men with her. She was going pretty fast, and she tooted her horn.

"Mr. Shotwell started to go forward, and then backward, he didn't seem to know how to get away, and the car knocked him down. There was a big crowd right away, and the machine stopped. A policeman they called Mike got in and made them drive him away."[46]

Perhaps Fitzgerald later recalled the grisly demise of his neighbor when writing *The Great Gatsby*. After Myrtle Wilson ran into the night and to her death in front of Gatsby's car, most of the witnesses told the police the car was "goin' thirty or forty miles an hour," but a "well-dressed Negro" contradicted them and said the car was going "faster'n forty."[47] Gatsby also perishes as a result of the accident. Similarly, in *This Side of Paradise,* Dick Humbird, a student at Princeton who "seemed the eternal example of what the upper class tries to be,"[48] dies in a car crash while driving back to the college from New York. In reality, Humbird's father is a grocery clerk; thus Humbird, like Gatsby, is a parvenu. A less significant example uniting automobiles and death occurs in the 1931 story "A New Leaf." One of the main characters, Dick Ragland, is said to have "killed somebody with an automobile. . . ."[49] Ragland also does not last until the end of the story; he drowns.

A more comical scene in Fitzgerald's fiction also ties cars to death. In *This Side of Paradise,* Amory plays Huck Finn to Myra's Aunt Sally as he tells a lie to cover up his failed attempt at being fashionably late to her party:

> "Well—I'll tell you. I guess you don't know about the auto accident," he romanced.
> Myra's eyes opened wide.
> "Who was it to?"
> "Well," he continued desperately, "uncle'n aunt'n I."
> "Was anyone killed?"
> Amory paused and then nodded.
> "Your uncle?"—alarm.
> "Oh, no—just a horse—a sorta gray horse."[50]

Scott's interest with the dangers of driving was not limited to his fiction. In 1935, he confessed to his cousin Ceci that his "great concern with Scottie [his dauther] for the next five years will be to keep her from being mashed up in an automobile accident."[51]

MISS STARK'S MANSLAUGHTER CASE was dismissed on June 10. The next day, the chief of police issued a warning to speeders who would "beat-it" down the streets at twenty-five or thirty miles an hour.[52] The police were also trying "to put a stop to the habit of young boys in the Hill districts stealing automobiles and taking joy rides. Many of the boys are said to belong to some of the best families and the police are handicapped by the fact that the automobile owners will not prosecute."[53]

The problem would not disappear by the time Fitzgerald and his friends grew fascinated by cars. They also took cars without permission and went for joy rides. Norris Jackson remembered motoring with Scott around the neighborhood. "I don't remember asking my parents if I could borrow the keys," he joked.[54] Stolen cars play a small role in Fitzgerald's first novel when Armory and some Princeton friends drive to the ocean, an adventure noted in Fitzgerald's *Ledger* for June 1914. "'You see,' said Kerry, 'the car belongs down there. In fact, it was stolen from Asbury Park by persons unknown, who deserted it in Princeton and left for the West.'"[55]

Another aspect of the lure of automobiles certainly came from their romantic potential. In the 1920s, automobiles provided young Americans another place to experience what passes for love, and Fitzgerald quickly realized the narrative potential. "When I was a boy I dreamed that I sat always at the wheel of a magnificent Stutz" he wrote in his *Notebooks*, "in those days the Stutz was the stamp of the romantic life."[56] With that in mind, Fitzgerald laces his stories and novels with front- and back-seat romances. Daisy shocks her husband out of his stupor when she suggests she drive with Gatsby into New York; Amory of *This Side of Paradise* convinces Myra to admit she cares for him in her chauffeured car; and Anthony first kisses Gloria in the back of New York taxi in *The Beautiful and Damned.*

Scott Fitzgerald's actual reputation with cars was more "Barney" Oldfield than Don Juan. Bob Clark remembered riding back to St. Paul with Fitzgerald from White Bear Lake. "I came home with him and I kept kicking the gear out. He was going too fast and was not quite in command."[57] One of Fitzgerald's characters, Basil Duke Lee, is only a couple years older than Scott was in 1910 when his grief at losing the wealthy Minnie Bibble in "He Thinks He's Wonderful" is palliated with the loan of his grandfather's electric car. He asks Imogene Bissel out for a drive. Her mother has forbidden her to ride with anyone under eighteen. "Does she mean an electric?" Basil asks. The answer comes: "Mother never heard of any wrecks in an electric." When Imogene agrees to go, Basil announces in a "reckless" voice: "I didn't mean that about this bus making only twelve miles an hour— it'll make fifteen. Listen, let's go down to Smith's and have a claret lemonade."[58]

CLUBS WERE VERY POPULAR WITH ADULTS at the turn of the century, and so naturally, young adults formed their own. Scott Fitzgerald and his Ramsey Hill friends were no exception. Perhaps the first organization Fitzgerald dreamed up was "The Cruelty to Animals Society," which came into existence in September 1908.[59] The club extended membership to both boys and girls but little was accomplished other than to gossip about dogs wandering through their backyards. Fitzgerald did adopt one of these strays and named him "The Duke of Del Monte." He also had another dog named "Blackie."[60] The club fizzled out when Fitzgerald resigned after being criticized for an unkind act by one of the other members.

Before long, more clubs were organized. Fitzgerald and his sometime rival Arthur Foley formed a detective club, known neither far nor wide as "The White Handkerchief."[61] Adolph

Schelle, George Gardner, Cecil Read, and Phil Foley soon joined. These six met secretly and quite irregularly in an old yellow house next to where Jack Mitchell once lived. Schelle was made president, and Fitzgerald had to settle for being secretary. Dues of five cents paid every two weeks were voted upon. Each boy was sworn to secrecy though none of them knew any secrets. With no prospects for any mysteries to solve, The White Handkerchief also folded.

The unemployed detective soon enlisted Cecil Read, Paul Baillon, and Harold Green to form a new organization: "The Boys Secret Service of St. Paul." Again Fitzgerald was not elected president, the honor being bestowed upon Baillon, perhaps because of his size and athletic ability. Fitzgerald was named chief scout; Read, chief spy; and Green, chief detective. Like its predecessors, this club soon faded into oblivion.

For a change of pace, Fitzgerald went into the lemonade business with Harold Green. It may have been just as exciting as their previous detective work and certainly was more rewarding.

The hiatus from club activity did not last long, and soon Fitzgerald and his companions were forming another secret society called "The Gooserah." This curious title was affixed upon the organization by accident. A boy in Scott's Sunday school class at St. Mary's church named Alfred Gusan caught the attention of the clique, and the jesting Paul Baillon exclaimed, "Rah for Goose Gooserah." The new organization even allowed the "Goose" to join, but only after surviving a rigorous initiation ceremony consisting of eating several raw eggs and allowing himself to be operated upon by Fitzgerald, Cecil Read, and Paul Baillon with their saws, needles and basins of ice.

"The Gooserah" was one of the more successful ventures, and soon Jim Porterfield, Sam Sturgis, Bob Clark, and Gus Schurmeier were taken into the fold. Cecil Read's house—a large brick structure one block north of Summit at 449 Portland—served as the meeting headquarters.[62] Meetings were held on the third floor while "maneuvers and operations" were conducted in the basement, which was referred to as the "gymnasium" by the youngsters. Here the tyro detectives engaged in a program of physical education to prepare their bodies to meet any test they might face.

There were three levels of membership. The "first degree" was bestowed upon anyone who survived initiation, and the "second degree" could be claimed by any officers. The "third degree" was awarded only to those who had rendered special services to the club.

In an attempt to expand the club, three new members were recruited: Donald Bigelow, Leonard Shepley, and McNeil Seymour. All three were members of the Ramaley Hall dance class. Influenced by the romance and violence of such groups as the Ku Klux Klan, the Gooserah organized an attack in April 1911 on Reuben Warner, one of Fitzgerald's rivals for the affections of the local lasses.[63] Mr. Warner called the police, who talked to Edward, who put an end to the club. (Scott used the episode in his short story "The Scandal Detectives." The hero of the story, Basil, is, of course, Fitzgerald. Ripley Buckner is Cecil Read, Bill Kempf is Paul Baillon, and Hubert Blair is Reuben Warner.) Although disbanded, it was not forgotten. Later, Cecil Read dubbed his yacht at White Bear Lake *The Gooserah.*

In July, Fitzgerald went to visit his uncle and aunt, Philip and Lorena McQuillan, at Bald Eagle Lake, just northwest of White Bear Lake. The train line, which parallels Highway 61 today, stopped at the station a few blocks from the lake at present day Buffalo Street. Many St. Paulites kept cabins between Buffalo Street and the lake or along East and Eagle Streets. Still others rented rooms at the Spring Lake Park Villa, a copy of the hotels on nearby White Bear Lake.[64] Visits to this resort area just a few miles north of St. Paul were a welcome change of pace from the city. The teen-aged Fitzgerald also spent time at Bob Clark's grandfather's house on Manitou Island, a narrow finger reaching out into the waters of White Bear Lake.[65] The exclusive community became Sherry Island in Fitzgerald's "Winter Dreams." Scott also stayed overnight with Cecil Read at Dellwood, another wealthy enclave on the shores of the lake. The two boys would lie awake at night listening to the rain beating on the roof while they discussed their plans for the future. Fitzgerald was already thinking of a Princeton education as he unraveled his dreams for Read.[66]

Spring Lake Park Villa, ca. 1910. (Courtesy Carroll Mattlin)

WHEN SCHOOL RECONVENED in September, the Fitzgeralds moved across the street into 509 Holly, vacated after the death of Stuart Shotwell. Scott entertained high hopes that he would finally make the football team that year. Even though he did manage to play sparingly at the end position, he tried out as the team's kicker. With adrenaline flowing and glory up for grabs, he botched an important kick in a big game. From then on, he busied himself as a statistician, keeping records of virtually anything connected with the game. For the rest of his life, Fitzgerald remained an avid sideline athlete. At the moment of his death, he was in Sheilah Graham's Hollywood apartment, "sitting in a green armchair, finishing a chocolate bar and making notes on an article in the Princeton *Alumni Weekly*: 'An Analytical Long Range View of the 1940 Football Team.'"[67]

Earlier that year, Scott was stricken by a crush on Donald Bigelow's sister, Alida. Miss Bigelow held the attention of many young men, and Fitzgerald and Bob Clark would often drop in on Donald with hopes of seeing Alida as well. These nocturnal gatherings at the Bigelow house at 415 Laurel became an almost nightly occurrence and did not taper off until Alida showed her favoritism for Arthur Foley and Egbert Driscoll.

With the resumption of Professor Baker's dancing instruction that fall, Fitzgerald's attentions focused on Marie Hersey and Margaret Armstrong. Marie, Scott admitted to himself, was the more attractive, but Margaret was the better talker, and to him the latter quality was more important than beauty. Because of Miss Armstrong's flair for words, he once told neighborhood friend Elisabeth Dean that Margaret was the most interesting person he knew.[68] She was extremely witty, and Scott was captivated by her outgoing personality.

Fitzgerald residence, 509 Holly. (Photo by Dave Page)

On the other hand, Marie Hersey made no attempt to conceal her affections for young Fitzgerald and even went so far as to reveal those feelings in a note she ordered hand-delivered to him by a friend. One midnight, Scott had a rendezvous with Cecil Read and Jim Porterfield on Ashland Avenue and, while confessing his own admiration for Marie, was overheard by Miss Suzanne Rice, who had been eavesdropping from her bedroom window. The following day, any secrets between Marie Hersey and Scott Fitzgerald were public domain.

Of course, the nascent author's budding affections were shifting almost daily. He was forever compiling lists of favorite girls, rating them by his own numerical system. He also rated his male companions and was regarded by his friends as a habitual note taker. According to St. Paul friend and Princeton classmate Norris Jackson, Fitzgerald continued the practice at the university. "He had a sort of thermometer that he rated people with," Norris remembered. "You even had to be someone to get on it."[69]

The 1910/1911 dancing class grew by four, three of whom were young ladies. Constance James of 654 Grand Avenue, Eleanor Alair of 708 Goodrich, and Margaret Winchester of 20 Kent Street became Professor Baker's enthusiastic new belles. The new boy was named William Landig. The addition of Eleanor Alair to the Ramaley School of Dance had been quite an accomplishment. In December 1910, the children at the school had presented a petition to Mrs. Townsend, who was now directing classes, asking to have Miss Alair join the class. Within a matter of days, their demand was met. With the success of the Alair petition, several of the dance pupils passed around another requesting to learn a new dance called "The Boston." The whims of the students were not met this time, so there was a rebellion when Arthur Foley, Cecil Read, Donald Bigelow and Larry Boardman refused to participate in the Grand March. An irate Professor Baker conducted the march without them, but the remainder of the class behaved so poorly that three new dances were introduced.

BESIDES DANCING CLASSES, the coming of winter meant more sleigh rides. In December, Joanne Orton assembled the dance class at her house for a bob. Margaret Armstrong and Marie Hersey, Fitzgerald's two favorites of the time, attended, so he was more than happy to go himself. That year was especially good for winter fun because the citizens of St. Paul had built an ice palace. The most spectacular castles had been constructed before the turn-of-the-century, but tradition kept the art alive and Fitzgerald was particularly struck by the beauty of the frozen spectacle. St. Paul is the only urban center in the United States which could claim such a monument, and only Moscow and Montreal also invested in these transitory displays.

Although the fortresses have been described by countless other observers and captured on photographic images, Fitzgerald's description in his classic story "The Ice Palace" is among the best memorials:

> After ten minutes they turned a corner and came in sight of their destination. On a tall hill outlined in vivid glaring green against the wintry sky stood the ice palace. It was three stories in the air, with battlements and embrasures and narrowed icicled windows, and the innumerable lights inside made a gorgeous transparency of the great central hall.[70]

Throughout the winter, Fitzgerald continued to try his hand at sports, practicing handball, boxing, and basketball, but he met with little success; he had more luck with the ladies. In midwinter the young Romeo had won the heart of Margaret Armstrong at a party given by Robert Clark. She invited him to a school dance at Oak Hall,[71] where they enjoyed themselves, but within a few months, Miss Armstrong's affection for Scott seemed to be disappearing. Trouble began in April when Julia Door assembled friends at her home at 561 Grand for a hike down the bluffs to Pleasant Avenue for a visit to "The ghost house. 'Down below the hill.'"[72] Two months earlier, Mrs. Emma Sebastian and her five children had claimed to see a "man with a black mustache, furry coat and wearing moccasins" in their home at 486 Pleasant.[73] So unnerved was Mrs. Sebastian that she moved from the house. No one might have noticed except for the fact that some bones, a crucifix and a rosary were found buried in the basement floor.

An inquest was called by the county attorney. The bones turned out to be those of a well-boiled, well-eaten pig, but the other artifacts could not be explained, so Miss Door and her friends could not resist a peek at the haunted house.

Dean House, 415 Summit Avenue. (Photo by Dave Page)

As the group paraded down the hill, Miss Armstrong shunned Fitzgerald in favor of Jim Porterfield, so the former did not share in the excitement when the gang reached its destination. On the return trip, Fitzgerald tried to interject himself into a conversation between Jim and Margaret, but without much success. A few days later, the rivals appeared together at the home of Elisabeth Dean at 415 Summit. Margaret Armstrong was also present, and the foursome slipped out for a walk. Soon Miss Armstrong and young Porterfield were a block ahead. Elisabeth raced ahead to Margaret, then returned to Fitzgerald with the news that he was still Margaret's favorite.

The following Friday, en route to Cecil Read's, Scott found Margaret and Elisabeth on a nearby corner. After a brief conversation, he escorted the former home, and the two talked for the first time since the haunted house trip. He asked her to attend a play and was elated when she accepted. The following day, Margaret telephoned to say she had to cancel, but Scott went anyway, determined to make the most of the performance.

Ames house, 501 Grand Hill. (Photo by Dave Page)

A fortnight after the play, Scott attended a party at Ben Griggs' house on Summit. He was elated to find Margaret present, as well as Marie Hersey, Dorothy Greene, Elisabeth Dean, Reuben Warner and Ted Ames. Having bested Jim Porterfield for Margaret's attentions, Scott was poised for success, but he was not prepared for what transpired that evening: Margaret ignored him again, this time in favor of Reuben Warner.

THE FAVORITE HANGOUT the spring and summer of 1911 was Ted Ames' backyard at 501 Grand Hill. Here flowers never ceased to bloom, and the deep shadows continually echoed with the laughter of children and the yapping of playful neighborhood canines.[74] Fitzgerald described the yard in his story "The Scandal Detectives" as a place where "there were deep shadows . . . all day long and ever something vague in bloom."[75]

The youngsters usually congregated at the base of a particularly giant oak tree. The sturdier boughs held a marvelous tree house with three floors. The bottom floor easily held eight youngsters who could whisper secrets and swear oaths of allegiance. The top floor was a secret known only to a few. In this attic hideaway, there lay "trunks of old clothes and costumes for dressing up."[76]

Sometimes the children would venture a block to the edge of the bluff where among the trees and rocks they would roast potatoes, eat apples or watch the bustling city below them. If things got a little too boring, the children would throw rocks toward the houses below.[77] "In sordid poverty," Fitzgerald writes in "The Scandal Detectives," "below the bluff two hundred feet away, lived the 'micks'—they had merely inherited the name, for they were now largely of Scandinavian descent—and when other amusements palled, a few cries were enough to bring a gang of them swarming up the hill, to be faced if numbers promised well, to be fled from into the convenient houses if things went the other way."[78]

Despite the apparent insensitivity of Fitzgerald's story, Scott later claimed:

> Like most Middle Westerners, I have never had any but the vaguest race prejudices—I always had a secret yen for the lovely Scandinavian blondes who sat on porches in St. Paul but hadn't emerged enough economically to be part of what was then society. They were too nice to be "chickens" and too quickly off the farmlands to seize a place in the sun, but I remember going round blocks to catch a single glimpse of shining hair—the bright shock of a girl I'd never know.[79]

Summers for Scott also meant weekly trips to the theater, much of the time with Gus Schurmeier. To add to the grown-up habit of smoking Fitzgerald had picked up in March, he began to wear his first long pants. The greatest excitement that spring, however, came from a decision by his family that he would attend Newman Academy in New Jersey the coming school term.

Perhaps faced with some sort of pressure to accomplish something memorable before he left St. Paul, Scott turned to drama. He had always been fond of playacting, and he and his friends used the attic of the Washington brownstone or the third-floor ballroom in the Read house as their private theaters. Scott would read the parts while Tubby Washington maneuvered cardboard figures and Cecil Read gave him script advice. In 1909, Fitzgerald organized a half-hour detective drama entitled *Arsène Lupin* in Teddy Ames' living room. During the next two years at St. Paul Academy, Scott participated in debate, recitations, and dramatic exercises, culminating in a May 12, 1911, performance during which he and Ted Ames "imitated stage personalities Montgomery and Stone singing 'Travel, Travel Little Star.'"[80] But his real break came that summer when Elizabeth Magoffin directed the neighborhood children in a theatrical hodgepodge at the school. Miss Magoffin—"a large, plump, enthusiastic girl in her mid-twenties"—oversaw St. Paul's Elizabethan Dramatic Club, the title referring to herself rather than the English queen.[81] During the August 8-9 benefit for the Protestant Orphan Asylum, Dorothy Greene and Fitzgerald performed a brief curtain raiser called *A Pair of Lunatics,* followed by Gus Schurmeier's magic tricks. The major attraction was a comedy called *A Regular Fix,* in which Fitzgerald held a minor role.[82]

Read house, 449 Portland.
(Photo by Dave Page)

Immediately after the extravaganza at St. Paul Academy, Scott completed a full-length play of his own, *The Girl from Lazy J.* With it, the young dramatist found a new audience. Despite the brief play's flaws, Elizabeth Magoffin recognized Fitzgerald's potential and allowed the melodramtic western to be presented in her home at 540 Summit. Tubby Washington gave Fitzgerald fits by not reading his lines correctly, but Miss Magoffin was able to soothe the playwright's ego: "To Scott," she wrote on a photograph, "'He had that spark—Magnetic mark'—with the best love of the one who thinks so."[83] With encouragement such as this, it is no wonder Scott penned "I begin to get my head turned," in his scrapbook.[84] Miss Magoffin and Fitzgerald would team up to produce a play every summer for the next three years.

THE COMING OF SEPTEMBER 1911 found the Fitzgerald family moving once again, just down the block to 499 Holly. As a sort of last hurrah, Fitzgerald and Cecil Read attended the Minnesota State Fair. As it still does today, the Great Minnesota Get-Together tempted young and old alike with bright lights, thrilling rides, exotic side-shows from around the world, and, best of all, an unending swarm of eligible young ladies, who, if they kissed, were called "chickens" by Scott and his friends.[85] The author captures the excitement in the opening paragraph of his short story "A Night at the Fair":

> The two cities were separated only by a thin well-bridged
> river; their tails curling over the banks met and mingled, and
> at the juncture, under the jealous eye of each, lay, every fall,

the State Fair. Because of this advantageous position, and because of the agricultural eminence of the state, the fair was one of the most magnificent in America. There were immense exhibits of grain, livestock and farming machinery; there were horse races and automobile races and, lately, aeroplanes that really left the ground; there was a tumultuous Midway with Coney Island thrillers to whirl you through space, and a whining, tinkling hoochie-coochie. As a compromise between the serious and the trivial, a grand exhibition of fireworks, culminating in a representation of the Battle of Gettysburg, took place in the Grand Concourse every night.[86]

With his long pants, published stories, produced plays, dreams of glory on the gridiron and his natural curiosity, Fitzgerald was ready to go East. Minnesota had left a deep impression and would continue to provide him with inspiration, but from then on he would call nowhere home for long, moving constantly to wherever exciting things were happening, a habit he had developed early in life. During those SPA years, his sister Annabel was playing with a neighbor girl on her back steps on Holly. Without warning, a lean, long-legged boy jumped from the porch, directly over their heads and rushed on his way. He was out of sight before they could catch their breaths. The astonished neighbor looked at Annabel, waiting for an explanation. Annabel met her gaze and answered: "That's Scott!"[87]

Notes

1 John Kuehl, ed., *The Apprentice Fiction of F. Scott Fitzgerald* (New Brunswick, N.J.: Rutgers University Press, 1965), 17.

2 Arthur Mizener, *The Far Side of Paradise* (New York: Avon Books, 1974), 44-45.

3 Jean Ingersoll Summersby. Letter to authors, 12 November 1976.

4 Kuehl, *Apprentice Fiction,* 29.

5 Jean Ingersoll Summersby. Telephone conversation with authors, 20 August 1976; Letter to authors, 12 November 1976.

6 Mrs. Richard Emmet, Jr. Letter to authors, 29 March 1979.

7 Robert D. Clark. Letter to authors, 17 May 1976.

8 Philip Stringer. Interview with authors. St. Paul, Minnesota, 1 March 1984; Jean Summersby. Telephone conversation with authors, 26 August 1976.

9 Stringer, Interview, 1 March 1984.

10 Jean Summersby. Telephone conversation with authors, 22 August 1976.

11 Elisabeth Dean Kennedy. Telephone conversation with authors, 15 August 1976.

12 Stringer. Interview, 1 March 1984.

13 Betty Ames Jackson. Interview with authors. St. Paul, Minnesota, 9 April 1983; Jean Ingersoll Summersby, Letter, 12 November 1976.

14 Beth Kent, "Fitzgerald's Back in Town," *The Grand Gazette,* August 1973, 7.

15 Nancy Milford, *Zelda* (New York: Harper & Row, 1970), 24.

16 Zelda Fitzgerald, *Save Me the Waltz* (New York: The New American Library, Inc., 1968), 45.

17 Mattthew Bruccoli, ed., *The Short Stories of F. Scott Fitzgerald* (New York: Charles Scribner's Sons, 1989), 376.

18 *Ibid.,* 230.

19 *Ibid.,* 31.

20 F. Scott Fitzgerald, *The Great Gatsby* (New York: Scribner Paperback Fiction, 1995), 6.

21 *Ibid.,* 113.

22 *Ibid.,* 13.

23 *Ibid.,* 15.

24 *Ibid.,* 141-142.

25 *Ibid.,* 185.

26 *Ibid.,* 112.

27 *Ibid.,* 187-188.

28 *Ibid.,* 116.

29 F. Scott Fitzgerald, *This Side of Paradise* (New York: Charles Scribner's Sons, 1970),18.

30 As an inside joke, Fitzgerald has the next person to speak wonder if it were Abraham Lincoln who said that a gentleman is one who never inflicts pain. The humor comes from the fact that it is the aforementioned Cardinal Newman who coined that definition. F. Scott Fitzgerald, *The Beautiful and Damned* (New York: Charles Scribner's Sons, 1922), 271-272.

31 *Gatsby,* 137.

32 J. Fetterley, "Introduction: On the Politics of Literature," from *The Resisting Reader,* 1977, in D. Herndl and R. Warhol, eds., *Feminisms: An Anthology of Literary Theory and Criticism* (New Brunswick, N.J.: Rutgers University Press, 1991), 385.

33 Benjamin Griggs. Interview with authors. St. Paul, Minnesota, 10 April 1976.

34 Beth Kent, "Fitzgerald's Back," 7.

35 Summersby. Letter, 12 November 1976.

36 Summersby. Telephone, 20 August 1976.

37 Elisabeth Dean Kennedy. Telephone conversation with authors, 15 August 1976; Robert D. Clark. Letter to authors, 17 May 1976.

38 Summersby. Telephone, 20 August 1976.

39 Andrew Turnbull, *Scott Fitzgerald* (New York: Charles Scribner's Sons, 1962), 23.

40 Summersby. Letter, 20 November 1976.

41 Fitzgerald, *Paradise*, 13.

42 Summersby. Letters, 12 & 20 November 1976; Philip Stringer. Interview with authors. St. Paul, Minnesota, 5 August 1976; 1 March 1984.

43 Summersby. Letters, 12 November 1976 and 4 November 1977.

44 F. Scott Fitzgerald, *The Basil and Josephine Stories* (New York: Charles Scribner's Sons, 1973), 89.

45 "Saints Drop Two Exciting Games to the Brewers at Lexington Park," *St. Paul Pioneer Press,* 23 May 1910, 6.

46 "Girl Autoist Kills Broker," *St. Paul Pioneer Press,* 23 May 1910, 1.

47 Fitzgerald, *Gatsby,* 147.

48 Fitzgerald, *Paradise,* 78.

49 Bruccoli, *Short Stories,* 635.

50 Fitzgerald,*Paradise,* 10-11.

51 Andrew Turnbull, ed., *The Letters of F. Scott Fitzgerald* (New York: Dell Publishing Co., Inc., 1966), 437.

52 "Last Hint to Autoists," *St. Paul Pioneer Press,* 11 June 1910, 2.

53 *Ibid.*

54 Margot Kriel, "Fitzgerald in St. Paul: People Who Knew Him Reminisce," in *University of Minnesota Conference on F. Scott Fitzgerald: Conference Proceedings,* 29-31 October, 1982, 25.

55 Fitzgerald, *Paradise,* 73.

56 Matthew Bruccoli, ed., *The Notebooks of F. Scott Fitzgerald* (New York: Harcourt Brace Jovanovich/Bruccoli Clark, 1978), 244.

57 Kriel, "Fitzgerald in St. Paul," 25.

58 Fitzgearld, *Basil and Josephine,* 98.

59 *Ledger,* 163.

60 F. Scott Fitzgerald, *Thoughtbook of Francis Scott Key Fitzgerald* (Princeton, N.J.: Princeton University Library, 1965). In *This Side of Paradise,* Amory has a dog named Count Del Monte.

61 Fitzgerald, *Thoughtbook.*

62 Robert D. Clark. Letter to authors, 5 July 1976; Clifton Read. Letter to authors, 3 December 1976; Emmy Lu Read ne Weed. Letter to authors, 1 January 1977. Cecil Read did not live on Holly Avenue when Fitzgerald knew him. Cecil's younger brother Clifton was born in the Portland Avenue residence in 1907, and their father passed away there in 1909. In 1911, the surviving Reads rented an apartment at 442 Summit, also the abode of Jim Porterfield, before moving into a rowhouse apartment at 123 Nina, part of the complex where Louisa McQuillan lived. Cecil and Emmy Lu Read did live on Holly Avenue in the 1950s, but that was long after Fitzgerald's death. Cecil's wife, who was born at 529 Holly, did recall Cecil living on Holly before the family moved to the Portland address, but that would have been Prior to the Fitzgeralds' return to St. Paul from Buffalo in 1908.

63 Mizener, *Paradise,* 16; *Ledger* 165.

64 Carroll Mattlin. Interview with authors. St. Paul, Minnesota, 11 December 1983.

65 Robert D. Clark. Letters, 24 April 1976, 17 May 1976, and 5 July 1976.

66 Clifton Read. Letter, 8 January 1977.

67 Jeffrey Meyers, *Scott Fitzgerald* (New York: HarperCollins Publishers, 1994), 333.

68 Elisabeth Dean Kennedy. Telephone conversation, 15 August 1976.

69 Norris Jackson. Interview at Lexington Avenue Library. St. Paul, Minnesota, 29 October 1982.

70 Bruccoli, *Short Stories,* 65.

71 Formerly the Backus' School for Girls.

72 *Ledger,* 165.

73 Oliver Towne, *St. Paul is My Beat* (St. Paul: North Central Pub. Co., 1958), 117.

74 Kent, "Fitzgerald's Back in Town," 7.

75 Fitzgerald, *Basil and Josephine,* 19.

76 Mrs. Richard Emmet, Jr., Letter, 29 March 1979.

77 Turnbull, *Scott Fitzgerald,* 19.

78 Fitzgerald, *Basil and Josephine,* 19.

79 Fitzgerald, *The Crack-Up,* 73.

80 Alan Margolies, ed., *F. Scott Fitzgerald's St. Paul Plays, 1911-1914* (Princeton, N.J.: Princeton University Library, 1978), 5.

81 Turnbull, *Scott Fitzgerald,* 42.

82 *Ledger,* 165; Margolies, *Plays,* 3.

83 Turnbull, *Scott Fitzgerald,* 42.

84 Margolies, *Plays,* 4.

85 Robert Clark. Letters, 24 April 1976 and 17 May 1976; *Ledger,* 166.

86 Fitzgerald, *Basil and Josephine,* 36-37.

87 Emmy Lu Read, ne Weed, Letter, 1 January 1977.

Chapter Five

Holiday Interludes
1911 to 1918

I N A 1934 LETTER to childhood sweetheart Marie Hersey, Fitzgerald claimed: "I no longer regard St. Paul as my home any more than the eastern seaboard or the Riviera."[1] However, the youthful Fitzgerald looked forward to the time he could spend in Minnesota. "One of my most vivid memories," reads a famous passage at the end of *The Great Gatsby*, "is of coming back west from prep school and later from college at Christmas time."[2] In fact, in a summary of the year 1911/1912 in his *Ledger*, Fitzgerald recalled that the year brought "real unhappiness excepting the feverish joys of Xmas."[3]

One of the reasons young Scott Fitzgerald enjoyed his trips back home was Marie Hersey. According to biographer Scott Donaldson, she was "Scott Fitzgerald's first girl. Not the first he noticed, or the first he kissed, but his first 'fixation,' as he put it, certainly his 'first love.'"[4] In his *Ledger*, Scott labels his 1911 Christmas visit to St. Paul "The Wonderful Vacation." He mentions Marie in connection with a drama club meeting and several holiday parties, including one at the Ames' house. As soon as he returned to Newman, he wrote to Elizabeth Magoffin to say that "Marie promised me her picture and I havn't [sic] gotten it yet."[5] And if Marie were not enough, there was always Margaret Armstrong, another young woman from his dance class, who, though not as pretty as Marie, was a better conversationalist.[6]

". . . the fact that they were starting away to school at the same time gave him a feeling of kinship for her—as if they had been selected for the glamorous adventure of the East, chosen together for a high destiny that transcended the fact that she was rich and he was only comfortable."
"A Night at the Fair"

Scott's abysmal performance at Newman provided him another reason to look forward to a break from classes. He had not distinguished himself academically, had struck out socially, and had failed to shine athletically. The best he could do, according to his *Ledger*, was make the "third football team. The scrubs."[7] His courage in one game was offset during a contest against Newark Academy when he avoided a tackle and gained the wrath of Charles "Sap" Donahoe, the quarterback of the Newman squad. At least in St. Paul, he could spend time with friends who admired and liked him.

When he returned to Newman in January, he brought with him an admonishment from his Aunt Annabel to put his nose to the grindstone. Unlike Aunt Clara, who had passed away the previous October and most nearly resembled Scott "in her fine blondness,"[8] Annabel did not spoil him, and she warned him not to read any trashy deviations from the standards. During the remainder of the school term, however, Fitzgerald managed to improve his scholastic standing at the school only slightly.

About the only thing that kept Scott focused while at Newman was his desire to attend Princeton. He had witnessed Princeton's defeat of Harvard the previous fall and was attracted to the idea of being a part of the Triangle Club, a group of students who yearly produced an original musical comedy. Inspired by his trips to New York City theater and his goal to succeed at Princeton, Scott drafted his second offering for Elizabeth Magoffin, *The Captured Shadow*, on the train ride back to St. Paul during the summer of 1912.

Newman School football team, Hackensack, New Jersey, 1912. F. Scott Fitzgerald is seated third from the left in the front row. (Courtesy of the Minnesota Historical Society)

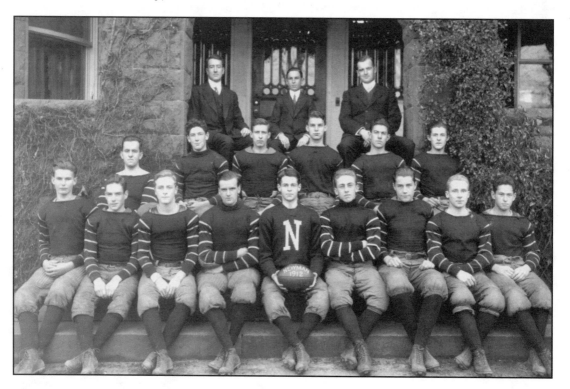

Mrs. Backus' School for Girls (Oak Hall), 580-590 Holly. (Photo by Dave Page)

Fitzgerald once again oversaw almost all aspects of the production of the mystery, even taking the lead role of the gentleman crook, Thornton Hart Dudley, The August 23, 1912, performance at Mrs. Backus' School for Girls (Oak Hall) on Holly Avenue, located just a short walk from the Fitzgeralds' home, unfolded in front of an appreciative audience of several hundred and elicited much favorable comment by "the young author's cleverness as well as by the remarkable amateur work acccomplished by the others of the cast."[9] In addition, the Baby Welfare Association grew richer by sixty dollars. The Schurmeiers, whose son Gus once again performed magic tricks on stage, hosted a cast dinner party the night before the show. After the curtain fell, the young thespians met at the Town and Country Club for a another party and supper.[10]

Fitzgerald later fictionalized the experience in one of his Basil Duke Lee stories, "The Captured Shadow." These nine stories based on his childhood between 1907 and 1913 were written between March 1928 and February 1929.[11] The *Saturday Evening Post* published all but one, thus sustaining Fitzgerald at a time when he was having trouble finishing his fourth novel.

The success of Fitzgerald's second Elizabethan Dramatic Club production was tempered by the young playwright's realization that his behavior could sometimes irritate people—"growing unpopular," he mused in his *Ledger* for July 1912.[12] Favorite pastimes for teens out of school included attending "Saturday night hops" at White Bear Lake, but getting to the resort city a dozen miles north of St. Paul could sometimes prove challenging. "Began to feel lack of automobile," Scott complained.[13]

Sixteen years later, Fitzgerald would fictionalize his lament in another Basil Duke Lee story, "He Thinks He's Wonderful." In the story, set in "the twelfth year of the century,"[14] the narrator decries: ". . . suddenly the great thing in Basil's crowd was to own an automobile."[15] Basil makes this observation after he has trouble getting to a dance at Black Bear Lake. He manages to convince some other boys to take him, but the three others ride in the front

White Bear Yacht Club, ca. 1910. (Author's collection)

and force Basil to sit in the back seat all alone.[16] Even worse, they plan a party and do not invite him. To get home, he begs another boy for a ride to Wildwood, where he can catch a streetcar back to St. Paul.

The actual Wildwood Park, an amusement complex located on the southeastern shore of White Bear Lake, had been constructed by the Twin City Rapid Transit Company in 1899 to give St. Paulites a reason to ride the company's Inter-Urban electric streetcars to White Bear Lake. From the park, steamboats would carry passengers to other points on the lake, such as the White Bear Yacht Club, scene of many summer dances.[17] The dances began precisely at 8:30 P.M. and would traditionally end with a rendition of "Home Sweet Home," a reminder to young people of the direction they should be taking. The last train from White Bear to St. Paul left promptly at 11:50 P.M.

Even if Scott proved to be conceited at times, it would not be long before he and his pals were making plans to return to White Bear Lake. Sometimes Scott and his friend Robert Clark would catch a streetcar to the park. A motorman stood at the controls and a conductor at the rear door by the post holding the coin deposit box. As the streetcar traveled through sparsely settled areas of North St. Paul, the motorman opened the throttle and the train sped along the tracks at what felt like "50 to 60 mph."[18] Once at Wildwood, the boys would ride the titanic roller coaster, listen to the merry-go-round or try their hands at games of skill.[19] Wildwood also boasted its own dance hall. For young squires like Scott and his friends, dances meant girls—young ladies to walk with, sometimes dance with, and in a few instances, ride home with.

If Scott's party returned home early enough, it might pass the lamplighter as he made his rounds, plodding along the streets in his horse-drawn cart with two high wheels. In the back of his cart were cans of kerosene that were emptied onto the top of the street lamps and then ignited. On Summit Avenue, where the lamps were more sophisticated, the lamplighter simply took out a key attached to the end of the long pole, turned the gas on in the lamps, then lit them.[20]

Sometimes transportation to and from the lake was not a problem, for Scott would spend entire weekends with Cecil Read in his parents' retreat on the lake. The White Bear Yacht Club was not far from the Read cottage, and Cecil's father had served as commodore of the club in 1905 and as vice commodore the previous year.[21] The Read place had four rooms on the main floor and four more on the second. The front porch, which offered a cool place to sleep, was wide and long. Another smaller sleeping porch extended from one side of the summer home. Behind the cottage was a small barn with a hayloft used by generations of youngsters as a playground. Scott and Cecil used the loft for meetings of whatever secret society they had happened to create that week.

Following some Saturday night dances, Scott and Cecil would slip back to the cottage and fall asleep on the porch, but not before talking until well past dawn. It was here, according to Clifton, Cecil's younger brother, that Scott confessed to Cecil after a yacht club dance his driving ambition to write a great Catholic novel.[22] Scott's sister sometimes visited the Read place with her brother. Annabel, whom the Reads considered to be the essence of charming femininity, taught Clifton how to dance.[23]

During many summer days at the lake, the pace actually slowed considerably. Robert Clark remembered that Scott was not much of a sailboat enthusiast nor much of a swimmer, perhaps because of a life-long reluctance to exhibit his feet.[24] Even so, Clark and Fitzgerald enjoyed wasting the summer days by lying on the beach just soaking up the sun.

Unlike Dexter Green, Scott's alter ego in "Winter Dreams," Scott never caddied at the White Bear Yacht Club and had very little interest in the game of golf, even though friends such as Dudley Mudge and Norris Jackson became quite good golfers. According to Clark, Scott preferred the glamour of the hard-hitting contact sports and served as a spectator at any golf outings.[25]

AUGUST DROPPED QUICKLY into September and the curtain fell on another summer in St. Paul. Scott's second season at boarding school was only a slight improvement over the first. He tried out once again for the football team and this time managed to gain recognition for his "fine running of the ball" in the *Newman News'* account of the game against Kingsley. Since Fitzgerald had just been named associate editor of the newspaper, the piece smacks of self-congratulations; nonetheless, he won a varsity letter in football that fall and another in track that spring.[26]

A decade later, he would recollect, "My two years [at Newman] were wasted, were years of utter and profitless unhappiness."[27] The few friends he made and his three published stories in the *News* could not offset his miserable academic and mediocre athletic performances. Perhaps to impress some classmates, he tried his first whiskey in March 1913 and got "tight" the next

month from "four defiant Canadian Club whiskeys at the Susquehanna in Hackensack."[28] The one highlight of Fitzgerald's second year at Newman was his acquaintance with Father Cyril
Sigourney Webster Fay, a Catholic convert with a private income
"who made the church seem glamorous."[29]

As he headed back to St. Paul for another summer, his
heart was set on attending Princeton that fall. His poor grades, miserable college board scores, and family's lack of money appeared
to be insurmountable obstacles, but Scott was not prepared to
accept the alternatives: matriculating at the University of Minnesota or Georgetown University, whose tuition his maiden aunt
Annabel had offered to pay. The death of his grandmother Louisa
McQuillan on July 15 that summer, a sad blow to the clan, did provide more than enough financial stability to ensure that Scott could
attend any college that would accept him. In his journal, Fitzgerald
wrote: "Grandmother dies. Her last gift."[30]

The funeral services were conducted July 17 at the
deceased's Laurel Avenue home, the same apartment at 294 Riley
Row where Scott had spent part of his own life.[31] Clergy at St.
Mary's Catholic Church, which had profited greatly from Louisa's
generous donations of time and money, laid her to rest in Calvary
Cemetery beside her husband, whom she had outlived by thirty-six
years.

The estate was equally divided among her four surviving
children: Allan, Philip, Annabel and Mollie. The total value was
tabulated at $116,609.60, comprising fifty shares in the McQuillan
Realty Company worth over $110,000, sixteen shares in the
Stockyards National Bank of South St. Paul valued at $2,400,
household goods valued at $1,000, and $1,568 owed to her by her
son Allan.[32]

ALTHOUGH SCOTT WROTE in his *Ledger* that he was "Studying for
Princeton,"[33] he seems to have spent most his summer completing

Fitzgerald's play *Coward*
held at YWCA in 1913.
(Courtesy of the Princeton
University Library)

another play for Elizabeth Magoffin, this one entitled *Coward*. Miss Magoffin maintained some semblance of order at rehearsals, but Fitzgerald kept the show going by the force of his personality:

> He knew how to soothe the girl who had only been able to rent one costume for a play whose action extended over several years. (Her mother had suggested her saying, "Here I am in the same old dress I was wearing when Sumter fell!") Then there was the girl who blushed at the line, "Father, remember your liver!" and the girl would wouldn't say the business about cleaning her nails because it was undignified.[34]

On August 29, 1913, the play was presented at the St. Paul YWCA with proceeds donated to the Baby Welfare Association. The profits of $150 were over double the amount taken the previous year. Fitzgerald shared the billing with friends Gustave Schurmeier—praised for his "careful study of the English . . . dialect"—and Laurance Boardman—called "the star" by reviewers—but it was once again Fitzgerald's show.[35] He portrayed Lieutenant Charles Douglas (one of the lead roles), switched to a minor role as a Union soldier, and was listed in the program as "Stage Manager."

An encore was given a few days later at the White Bear Yacht Club before an audience of 300.[36] Prior to the show, Mr. and Mrs. Worrell Clarkson of Dellwood hosted a dinner at the club in honor of the young actors and actresses.[37] During the actual performance, Fitzgerald had to ad-lib when a props person standing off-stage realized that the gun with which he was supposed to fire a blank was actually loaded with a live round. The frightened extra ran down three flights of stairs and out to the end of the dock before blasting at the stars. In the meantime, Scott rummaged for a box of cigars. In another more comical moment, one of the actors said, "Here comes Father now," and pointed to stage left; whereupon the old man in his wheelchair hurtled in from the right.[38]

"EVERYONE SAYS YOU'RE FOOLISH to go [to college] at sixteen," a friend tells Basil in Fitzgerald's short story "Forging Ahead."[39] Basil replies, "I'll be seventeen in September," and just like his creator, heads East. Any conceit sixteen-year-old Scott Fitzgerald felt about his chances on the make-up exams was unfounded. His efforts fell short. Determined not to accept failure, he went personally before the admissions committee and pleaded with the members not to cast him from the school on his seventeenth birthday. The committee reconsidered, and on September 24, Fitzgerald wired his parents to SEND FOOTBALL PADS AND SHOES IMMEDIATELY.[40] He still hoped sports would catapult him to collegiate fame.

In "Pasting It Together," written for *Esquire* in 1936, Fitzgerald admitted his shoulder pads were only "worn for one day on the Princeton freshman football field. . . ."[41] To a different audience, the 138-pound Fitzgerald claimed he managed through three days of drills before leaving with a badly sprained ankle.[42] In *This Side of Paradise,* Amory lasts until the second week of practice, when he "wrenched his knee seriously enough to put him out for the rest of the season."[43]

In the same novel, Fitzgerald writes about catching sight of the captain of the Princeton football squad while out walking with friends. St. Paul acquaintance and Princeton classmate Norris Jackson, whom Fitzgerald affectionately called Nonnie, remembered a similar scene when St. Paul native Joe McKibbin stopped by Jackson's room with another senior.

> Scott and my friend Henry Dunley were there in the room and Joe said: "How 'bout we all take a walk?" So we did. Walked down through campus and then along the canal, a nice sort of place. Scott was feeling very relaxed and sort of skipped around or went over and knocked an apple off a tree or something like that.[44]

Later, Scott burst into Jackson's room asking if he knew the upperclassmen who happened by the room that night. Jackson said of course he knew. It was Joe McKibbin. "Yea," Scott replied, "but do you know who the senior was? He's the captain of the football team and plays tackle. And I acted just like a damn fool."

The senior's name was Hobart "Hobey" Baker, one the few Princeton demi-gods who would actually fraternize with freshmen. "Scott was anxious," Jackson insisted, "really and truly anxious, to know important people and have a chance to be with people he thought important. Scott was outraged that he had made, perhaps, a bad impression. . . ." Just a handful of years later, Baker would join the 103rd Squadron, the famous Lafayette Escadrille during World War I and fly a spad painted Princeton orange and black. He met an untimely death during his final flight on December 21, 1918.[45]

By his 1913 Christmas break, Scott had fostered a reputation for being "fast" with the girls and drinking.[46] While some of the notoriety was deserved, he did tend to exaggerate the claims. According to an article he wrote a decade later, he was suppering with friends that holiday season a few doors from St. John's Episcopal Church, still located on the corner of Portland and Kent. (The Ordways, friends of Fitzgeralds', lived just east of the church.) The sanctuary was filled with the ranks of St. Paul aristocracy when a tipsy Fitzgerald entered looking for a familiar face with whom he could sit and join in the singing of hymns. The amazed congregation stared as he swayed up the aisle, his overshoe buckles clinking all the way to the pulpit, where he told a surprised clergyman to continue the service and pay him no heed. The St. Paul papers, Fitzgerald claimed, had "an extra out before midnight."[47] In fact, no such account exists. Furthermore, according to his own list of activities that holiday season, he spent Christmas Eve at his aunt's.[48]

In addition to visiting his Aunt Annabel, Fitzgerald did manage to attend a few parties and socialize at the University Club.

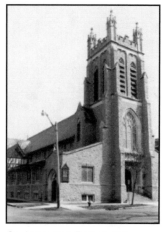

St. John the Evangelist Episcopal Church, Portland and Kent. (Photo by Dave Page)

Opened the previous year at 420 Summit, where the elm-lined boulevard flexes its elbow, the University Club evolved from the outdated St. Paul Club, formerly at 102 Western Avenue. Scott was never an official member, but his father was, even though membership was supposed to be restricted to university graduates.[49] Throughout his last few years in St. Paul, Scott attended many social functions there and utilized the V-shaped building towering over St. Paul and the Mississippi River as a setting for many of his stories. Legend has it that he even carved his name in a downstairs bar, but one University of Minnesota student who spent three days looking for the elusive autograph never found it.[50]

Back at Princeton, he was busy with the Triangle Club holiday show and was rewarded for his efforts with election to a full membership in the club. Given the choice, Scott decided to forego his studies. "He didn't hit the books," recalled Jackson.[51] He collected quite a few blue-colored deficiency reports, a disgrace recalled in *This Side of Paradise*. Undaunted, Scott spent the rest of winter writing a script for the following year's Triangle Christmas show. He learned in March he had won the competition.

Buoyed by his successes at Princeton and fascinated by political events in Europe, Scott returned to St. Paul during the summer of 1914. He was visiting his Uncle Philip McQuillan when World War I broke out. As could be expected, the front pages of the *St. Paul Pioneer Press* were filled with stories of bitter fighting. The paper also ran a brief article about the centenary of the writing of "The Star Spangled Banner" and mentioned that Edward Fitzgerald, a distant relative of Francis Scott Key, would be unable to join the other St. Paul delegates of the Baltimore Celebration.[52] He may have decided to remain in St. Paul because

University Club, 420 Summit Avenue, 1982. (Photo by Dave Page)

Elizabethan Dramatic Club to Play For Benefit of Baby Welfare Fund

MEMBERS of the cast of the play, "Assorted Spirits," to be presented Tuesday evening at the Y. W. C. A. auditorium under the auspices of the Y. W. C. A. Left to right, upper picture, Elynor Alair, Alice Lyon, Dorothy Greene, Katherine Schulze, Margaret Armstrong, Betty Mudge. Below, McNeil Seymour, Robert Clark, Scott Fitzgerald, Gustav Schurmeier, John Mitchell and Joseph B. Armstrong.

St. Paul Pioneer Press article about Fitzgerald's Elizabethan Dramatic Club. (Used with permission)

his son's fourth and final show for the Elizabethan Dramatic Club was to open the same week as the Baltimore gathering.

Scott's last script for Miss Magoffin is called *Assorted Spirits*, a literal play on the two meanings of the word: supernatural and hard liquor. The play tells the story of Josephus Hendrix who tries to depreciate the value of a house he wishes to purchase by making the owners believe it is haunted. The curtain went up September 8 before an enthusiastic full house at the St. Paul YWCA auditorium, earning another $300 for the Baby Welfare League. The reviewer for the *St. Paul Pioneer Press* indicated that Fitzgerald had turned out a "roaring farce" and did a "good" job acting the role of Peter Weatherby, an old man.[53]

Because some had to be turned away the first night, a second performance was staged at the White Bear Yacht Club the following night. Although no admission was charge, another $200 was added to the coffers of the Baby Welfare League through donations but not before Fitzgerald averted tragedy when a fuse blew and plunged the audience of 200 into darkness. According to an article in the *Daily News,* he "calmed the audience in a neat impromptu speech and held its attention until the lights were repaired."[54] The *St. Paul Pioneer Press* reported that the audience was almost in a panic when the the seventeen-year-old playwright leaped to the edge of the stage and "quieted the audience with an improvised monolgue."[55]

The little time remaining in his busy schedule was spent being tutored for a make-up test in geometry. His failure to pass the test that fall made him ineligible to appear in his Triangle Club play, *Fie! Fie! Fi-Fi!* Still, he spent the fall helping to perfect the production. In it he introduced audiences to a literary creation that would fuel his imagination and pocketbook for the next decade and a half: the flapper. "I had no idea of originating an American flapper when I first began to write," he said in a 1923 interview. "I simply took the girls whom I knew very well and, because they interested me as unique human beings, I used them for my heroines. . . ."[56]

Unable to tour with the show, he returned to St. Paul for Christmas break somewhat of a celebrity. On his last night home, he met one of the Ivy League's "Big Four" debutantes, a flapper's flapper. Her name was Ginevra King, and she would provide inspiration for Fitzgerald's fiction the remainder of his life, "the stamp that goes into my books so that people can read it blind like Braille."[57]

Marie Hersey, Ginevra's roommate at Westover, invited the dark-haired, dark-eyed beauty to spend the holidays in St. Paul. In honor of her visit, a bob-sledding party was initiated by Elizabeth McDavitt on January 4, 1915. For Miss Hersey and the other young elites of the Summit Hill neighborhood, the event was one of the highlights of the holiday season, and the affair was duly chronicled in the society pages of a St. Paul newspaper.

Miss King came from a wealthy Chicago family, and Marie Hersey had passed along socialite gossip about Miss King to Fitzgerald. As early as July 1911, Fitzgerald had noted in his *Ledger* the name Ginevra King. "Again the name Ginevra" he echoed in January 1913. She was known to dangle beaus upon strings wherever she traveled, and in addition was supposed to be an affable conversationalist and excellent dancer.

The St. Paul festivities in honor of Ginevra got underway with a sleigh ride to the Town and Country Club, where a customary cup of hot chocolate awaited. Then the party returned to the McDavitt home at 596 Grand for dinner. Even though "the McDavitt house on Grand never was much—it was on the wrong street"[58]—all the Summit Hill gentry were there.[59] However, it was Fitzgerald who most captivated Miss King. She promised to see

Ice palace at Town and Country Club, ca. 1915. (Courtesy Town and Country Club)

McDavitt house, 596 Grand Avenue, 1990. (Photo by Dave Page)

him again out East, but after Fitzgerald left St. Paul for Princeton, she shifted her attentions to his old nemesis Reuben Warner.

Fitzgerald tried throughout the next year to fan the flames of Ginevra's desire, but he was rarely more than a name on a list. Even if he made it to the top on occasion, her feelings for him were never "serious enough not to want plenty of other attention."[60] Yet it was Ginevra who would gain immortality in Fitzgerald's prose, as Rosalind Connage in *This Side of Paradise*, Judy Jones in "Winter Dreams," Daisy Buchanan in *The Great Gatsby* (Ginevra's friend Edith Cummings was Jordan Baker[61]), Nicole Diver in *Tender is the Night*, Josephine Perry in the Josephine stories, and a dozen or more other young women in Fitzgerald's works.

Back at Princeton, Scott carried on passionate correspondence with Ginevra while he collaborated with Edmund Wilson on the next production for the Triangle Club, *The Evil Eye*. At the end of February, he was elected secretary of the club and was well on his way to becoming one of the really big men on campus. Needless to say, his academic performance continued to suffer: "In chemistry class," classmate Norris Jackson joked, "he would rather cook eggs than do the experiments."[62]

After a brief visit to Lake Forest, Illinois, to see Ginevra at the beginning of summer break in 1914, Scott loitered in St. Paul for a month at his parents' new abode at 593 Summit, a quite respectable rowhouse on the most prestigious street in St. Paul. He then accepted an invitation from Princeton classmate Charles "Sap" Donahoe to enjoy the last warm months at his parents' ranch in Montana. By summer's end, "it seemed as though he had finally reached the summit of that popularity toward which he had struggled so long and with such determination."[63] But the triumph was a mirage.

Upon his return to Princeton, he learned that he was again ruled ineligible for extra-curricular activities because of a poor record his sophomore year. He had flunked one term of sophomore Latin and both terms of sophomore chemistry. A committee of Triangle associates petitioned the dean to allow Fitzgerald to perform in the club's show since his photograph had appeared in newspapers from New York to Minnesota, but the appeal failed. Fitzgerald took ill, and returned to St. Paul to convalesce.

Princeton orange and black decorated store fronts in Minneapolis and St. Paul as the long-awaited Triangle Club Christmas show arrived in the Twin Cities for the first time on December 28, 1915. When the hometown curtain went up on *The Evil Eye*, it seems that Fitzgerald may have been on stage. An article in the next day's *St. Paul Dispatch* asked the two hometown boys in the production what it felt like to play girls. "Scott Fitzgerald of St. Paul, who wrote the lyrics for 'The Evil Eye' is much too polite to say he does not enjoy being a girl, but neither will he admit he doesn't think it fun," the reporter wrote. The second native was Laurance Boardman, another one of the actors in the Elizabethan Dramatic Dlub.[64]

Also during the holidays, Fitzgerald escorted Marie Hersey to a dance at the Summit Avenue mansion belonging to Louis Hill, son of empire builder James J. Hill. Fitzgerald had turned down other invitations that holiday season, but the combination of Marie's charms and the Hill mystique helped to pull him out socially.

Perhaps in an attempt to improve his health, Scott tried to cut back on smoking. By February, he was well enough to take a short trip to Princeton where he was informed—not unexpectedly—that he would have to repeat his junior year. Upon returning to St. Paul, he lived with his Aunt Annabel a short time. As a spoof, he masqueraded as a young lady, complete with dress and makeup, and attended a Psi Upsilon dance at the University of Minnesota on February 26. Gustave Schurmeier's sister, Mrs. J.M. Hannaford, Jr., provided Fitzgerald with the feminine apparel, and Gus acted as escort to the fraternity house, located at 1721 University Avenue S.E.[65] If he couldn't be the most beautiful show girl in the

Top right: Psi Upsilon Fraternity. (Courtesy of the University of Minnesota archives)

Above: Triangle Club Publicity photo of F. Scott Fitzgerald. (Author's collection)

Triangle Club, at least he could act the part in another venue. As a "stunning blonde in a turquoise gown," Fitzgerald spent the evening casually asking for cigarettes in the middle of the dance floor and absent-mindedly drawing a small vanity case from the top of a blue stocking.[66] Freshmen were forced to take walks outside to cool themselves, while Fitzgerald filled his dance card with the names of "all the popular fraternity men and best dancers."

One version of the escapade has Fitzgerald escaping unde-tected after beguiling several male party goers into requesting a later rendezvous. Another suggests that Scott was caught when he tried to enter the men's restroom. In any event, the escapade made the front page of the following Monday's *St. Paul Daily News*. "Mr. Fitzgerald, who is a Princeton student, at home on leave of absence," the article ended, "has made a name for himself in col-lege circles as an extremely successful female impersonator."

The coming spring marked a turning point in Fitzgerald's writing career. He tried to promote an idea for the next Triangle Club production, but it was turned down. His disappointment at the rejection and his lack of any chance to be the next Triangle president discouraged him from pursuing a career in theater. Al-though he had offers from New York agents who suggested he leave college and try his luck on Broadway,[67] he decided to return to Princeton in the fall, even if it meant joining the class of 1918. In the meantime, he began work on "Spires and Gargoyles," what he called "the beginning of mature writing."[68] The short story "The Spire and the Gargoyle" appeared in the February 1917 *Nassau Lit*, but the *Ledger* reference may have been to a chapter title in *This Side of Paradise.*

As soon as the snow began to melt, Edward Fitzgerald acquired a second-hand Chalmers. The automobile was not very fast. Even so, Scott managed to coax enough speed out of it so that at least one friend would kick it out of gear in order to slow him down.[69] He taught his friend and Princeton classmate Nonnie Jackson to drive and took trips out to the White Bear Yacht Club, where his father was now a member.[70] Besides nipping apple brandy in the locker room,[71] he finally tried his hand at golf. Even so, he was much more interested in dancing: "He spent hours before the mirror practicing the Maxixe, the Turkey Trot, and the Aeroplane Glide."[72]

Scott's decision to curtail his own career in theater did not dampen his enthusiasm for drama. He again wrote lyrics for the 1916/1917 Triangle show, *Safety First,* and saw his own play about Ginevra, *The Debutante,* published in the January 1917 issue of Princeton's *Nassau Lit* magazine. In addition, throughout his convalescence in St. Paul, Fitzgerald continued his boyhood habit of attending plays. In late spring he invited two actresses from a road company to go dancing with him and a friend after their performance. They accepted, and Scott had a chance to use his skills as a hoofer. The next afternoon, the foursome lunched at the University Club, raising quite a few eyebrows.[73]

The illness that had prompted Scott to drop out of Princeton seems to have dragged on into the summer of 1916 since Fitzgerald took what he called an "ill-fated health trip to Brainerd" in July.[74] What was "ill-fated" about his trip to Northern Minnesota is not recorded, but his destination may have been a sanitarium for tuberculosis patients just twelve miles out of town.[75] In 1929, Fitzgerald was examined by a radiologist as part of an application for an insurance policy. The X-rays confirmed that Fitzgerald had indeed suffered from tuberculosis, but the doctor assured him it was not an active case.[76]

If poor health was to kill him that summer, it would be his heart and not his lungs. Scott traveled to Lake Forest in August only to bemoan in his *Ledger,* "Poor boys shouldn't think of marrying rich girls."[77] If Ginevra's father, Charles King, had not said the line, he certainly thought it. King, his polo ponies, and his departure from Chicago for Long Island provided Fitzgerald with the model for Tom Buchanan in *The Great Gatsby.*[78]

"A year of terrible disappointments and the end of all college dreams," Fitzgerald summarizes in his *Ledger.* "Everything bad was my own fault."[79]

SCOTT ENTERED PRINCETON that fall as a junior with only a small hope he could resurrect his flagging college career. By October he was again ruled ineligible for the Triangle show and contented himself by taking Marie Hersey to the Christmas opening. After the holidays, he learned he had again come close to flunking out of school, and he gave serious thought to joining the widening war in Europe. Some of his closest St. Paul friends had volunteered. Cecil Read, Robert Clark, Donald Bigelow and "Mac" Seymour were all training in the Air Field Service or Lafayette Esquadrille.[80]

As usual, academics took a back seat to other pursuits, but this year work on *Lit* stories, poems, and book reviews—thirteen appearances in all—superseded his involvement in Triangle activities. Fitzgerald's meeting with Ginevra in St. Paul inspired one of the more notable efforts of that period, "Babes in the Woods," published in the May 1917 issue of *Nassau Lit* and eventually incorporated into *This Side of Paradise.*

When school let out in June, he visited Father Fay at his mother's home in Deal Beach, New Jersey. The priest wanted Scott to accompany him on a diplomatic trip to Russia. Scott was

Building 53, Post Gymnasium, Fort Snelling, 1983. (Photo by Dave Page)

intrigued by the offer but decided to prepare an alternative in case the plan failed to materialize. In July, he returned to his parents' apartment at 593 Summit in St. Paul and took exams for an infantry commission at Fort Snelling. While he awaited the results, he attended a "Russia Dance" at the post.[81] These social gatherings for students at the officers' training camp commenced earlier that year, and although there were many YMCA-sponsored events held in the post chapel, the officers' dances were held in Building 53, the post gymnasium, a red brick building constructed in 1903. As enjoyable as the company of young women was, many of the aspiring officer candidates, such as Fitzgerald, spent their time asking those who had already been through military training what it was like—and the number of those with personal experience in the rigors of camp was skyrocketing. As America prepared to enter the conflict overseas, Fort Snelling expanded at a rapid pace to handle the new influx, adding 215 new buildings.[82]

Fitzgerald was not the only literary heavyweight residing on Summit Avenue in late summer 1917. Piloting his new Hupmobile into town, Sinclair Lewis and his wife, Grace, rented a home one block from Scott's parents' apartment. Lewis called 516 Summit Avenue the "lemon meringue pie" house because its yellow brick exterior was spotted with dabs of whipped cream marble. The home was the scene of many parties to which the hosts invited both wealthy industrialists and Farmer-Labor liberals. Although living practically across the street from one another, Lewis and Fitzgerald did not meet at this time. Not unexpectedly, Lewis fell afoul of Summit Avenue politics when he refused to discharge his German nurse after America's entry into World War I. He became even more of an outcast for his support of Fritz Kreisler, the famous violinist who was sending money to wounded Austrians. Lewis' involvement with socialist groups in Minnesota added more ammunition to his detractors, and he was pressed into leaving town rather suddenly on March 27, 1918.[83]

When Father Fay's Russian adventure was canceled in

Sinclair Lewis house, 516 Summit Avenue. (Photo by Dave Page)

September, Fitzgerald returned to Princeton to await his expected commission. His Princeton transcripts list no courses for the term, but he continued editorial work on the *Tiger* humor magazine and the *Lit* and had his first professional acceptance from *Poet Lore* magazine, but "The Way of Purgation" was never published.[84] Though ending their relationship once and for all the previous summer, Ginevra remained Scott's inspiration. In "The Pierian Springs and the Last Straw," published in the October issue of the *Lit*, the middle-aged hero loses his Ginevra as a young man and never gets over it.

On November 14, Scott's commission came through and he was ordered to Fort Leavenworth, Kansas, to commence the three-month Officers' Candidate School. His spare time was devoted to furious work on his novel. Tentatively titled *The Romantic Egotist*, it was a patchwork of pieces in several different genres, some already published. More than once he had to be reprimanded by superiors for scribbling on his novel while he was supposed to be taking lecture notes. One of the officers that oversaw his military education was a future commanding general and president, Dwight D. Eisenhower.[85]

When Fitzgerald received leave in February, he hurried to Princeton and finished his novel at Cottage Club before mailing it off to his friend, the author Shane Leslie, who in May passed the manuscript on to his publisher, Charles Scribner's Sons. Leslie's note accompanying the novel read "when [Fitzgerald] is killed, it will have commercial value."[86]

Fitzgerald passed through Camp Taylor near Louisville, Kentucky, on his way to Camp Gordon in Georgia. In June, his regiment was combined with a regiment at Camp Sheridan near Montgomery, Alabama, where he received his promotion to first lieutenant. The next month he encountered a real Southern belle, Miss Zelda Sayre, at a country club dance. Fitzgerald's moth just met another flame.

Notes

1 Andrew Turnbull, ed., *The Letters of F. Scott Fitzgerald* (New York: Dell Publishing Co., Inc., 1963), 536.

2 F. Scott Fitzgerald, *The Great Gatsby* (New York: Scribner Paperback Fiction, 1995), 183.

3 *F. Scott Fitzgerald's Ledger: A Facsimile* (Washington, D.C.: A Bruccoli Clark Book, 1972), 166.

4 Scott Donaldson, *Fool for Love* (New York: Congdon & Weed, Inc., 1983), 43.

5 Matthew Bruccoli and Margaret Duggan, eds., *Correspondence of F. Scott Fitzgerald* (New York: Random House, 1980), 5.

6 Donaldson, *Fool,* 44.

7 *Ledger,* 166.

8 Andrew Turnbull, *Scott Fitzgerald* (New York: Ballantine Books, 1971), 36.

9 "Play Helps Babies," *The St. Paul Pioneer Press,* 24 August 1912, 9.

10 Alan Margolies, *F. Scott Fitzgerald's St. Paul Plays, 1911-1914* (Princeton, N.J.: Princeton University Library, 1978), 6.

11 F. Scott Fitzgerald, *The Basil and Josephine Stories by F. Scott Fitzgerald* (New York: Charles Scribner's Sons, 1973), vii.

12 *Ledger,* 166.

13 *Ledger,* 166.

14 Fitzgerald, *Basil,* 77.

15 Fitzgerald, *Basil,* 86.

16 In his *Ledger,* 170, Fitzgerald seems to place the actual incident in July 1916: "Ride alone with. . . . Me in back seat."

17 Nancy Woolworth, *The White Bear Story* (White Bear Lake: N.P., 1975), 36-46.

18 "Readers share memories of Twin Cities railway transit," *St. Paul Pioneer Press,* 4 March 1995, 7A.

19 Robert Clark. Letter to authors, 17 May 1976.

20 Reuben L. Zabel, "Early Summit Avenue grace and elegance are part of his past," *St. Paul Dispatch,* 28 May 1979, 8.

21 Drake, Carl B., et al., *The White Bear Yacht Club: Its History* (St. Paul: Bruce Publishing Co., 1961), 141.

22 Clifton Read. Letters to authors, 3 December 1976 and 8 January 1977.

23 In 1922, Fitzgerald's last year in Minnesota, the Reads sold the cottage. It was moved across winter ice and joined with another cottage to make a substantial home for the new owners. The combined structure still exists, but has little resemblance to its original appearance.

24 *Ledger,* 155.

25 Robert D. Clark. Letter to authors, 17 May 1976.

26 Henry Dan Piper, *F. Scott Fitzgerald: A Critical Biography* (New York: Holt, Rinehart and Winston, 1965), 18.

27 Piper, *Fitzgerald,* 19.

28 Matthew Bruccoli and Jackson Bryer, eds., *F. Scott Fitzgerald: In His Own Time* (New York: Popular Library, 1971), 223. He noted in an April *Ledger* entry that he was "Tight at Susquehanna." *Ledger,* 167.

29 Bruccoli, *Epic Grandeur,* 36.

30 *Ledger,* 167.

31 "Funeral of Mrs. M'Quillan," *St. Paul Pioneer Press,* 16 July 1913, C11.

32 The will of Louisa McQuillan is on file at the Ramsey County Courthouse, St. Paul, Minnesota.

33 *Ledger,* 167.

34 Turnbull, *Scott Fitzgerald,* 42.

35 "Coward' at Y.W.C.A. Pleases a Large Crowd," *The St. Paul Pioneer Press,* 30 August 1913, 4.

36 Margolies, *Fitzgerald's Plays,* 7.

37 Bruccoli, *Romantic Egoists,* 18.

38 Turnbull, *Scott Fitzgerald,* 43.

39 Fitzgerald, *Basil ,* 146.

40 Bruccoli, *Romantic Egoists,* 20.

41 F. Scott Fitzgerald, *The Crack-Up* (New York: New Directions Book, 1945), 84.

42 Turnbull, *Scott Fitzgerald,* 44.

43 Fitzgerald, *Paradise,* 43.

44 Norris Jackson. Interview at St. Paul Lexington Avenue Library. St. Paul, Minnesota, 19 October 1982.

45 John Davies, *The Legend of Hobey Baker* (Boston: Little, Brown and Company, 1966), xvi.

46 Piper, *Fitzgerald,* 19.

47 Bruccoli, *In His Own Time,* 234.

48 Bruccoli, *Romantic Egoists,* 20.

49 Donaldson, *Fool,* 19.

50 Dave Page, "F. Scott and Zelda in St. Paul," *City Pages,* 29 September 1982, 8.

51 Norris Jackson. Interview at St. Paul Lexington Avenue Library. St. Paul, Minnesota, 29 October 1982.

52 "Francis Key Honor Near," *St. Paul Pioneer Press,* 3 September 1914, 11.

53 "Play Nets $300 for Baby Welfare Fund," *St. Paul Pioneer Press,* 9 September 1914, 14.

54 "Assorted Spirits Played for Charity," *St. Paul Daily News,* 10 September 1914, 5.

55 "Lights Contribute Thrill to Playlet," *St. Paul Pioneer Press,* 10 September 1914, 12.

56 Bruccoli, *In His Own Time, 265.*

57 Bruccoli, *Romantic Egoists,* 27.

58 Mrs. Richard Emmet, Jr. Letter to authors, 29 March 1979.

59 The party included Alida Bigelow, Katherine Ordway, Marie Hersey, Mary Johnston, Grace Warner, Betty Mudge, Constance James, Betty Foster, Eleanor Alair, Mary Butler, Joanne Orton, Vernon Rinehart, Frank Hurley, Reuben Warner, Gustave Schurmeier, Laurance Boardman, William Lindeke, Robert Barton, James Armstrong, James Porterfield, Robert Dunn, Harrison Johnston, Ginevra and Scott.

60 Donaldson, *Fool,* 49.

61 Bruccoli, *Epic Grandeur,* 216.

62 Norris Jackson. Interview at St. Paul Lexington Avenue Library. St. Paul, Minnesota, 29 October 1982.

63 Piper, *Fitzgerald,* 20.

64 The papers often spelled Boardman's Christian name as "Lawrence." Jane Grey, "It's Great to be a Girl—For Three Hours Only," *St. Paul Dispatch,* 29 December 1915, 5.

65 The building now houses the University of Minnesota Students' Co-op.

66 "Stunning Blond Stuns 'U' Men," *St. Paul Daily News,* 28 February 1916, 1.

67 Piper, *Fitzgerald,* 23.

68 *Ledger,* 170.

69 Turnbull, *Scott Fitzgerald,* 68.

70 Donaldson, *Fool,* 11.

71 Bruccoli, *In His Own Time,* 223.

72 Turnbull, *Scott Fitzgerald,* 68-69.

73 *Ibid.,* 69.

74 *Ledger,* 170.

75 Roseann Sanders. Letter to authors, 12 February 1984.

76 Bruccoli, *Epic Grandeur,* 272.

77 *Ledger,* 170.

78 Richard Lehan, *The Great Gatsby: The Limits of Wonder* (Boston: Twayne Publishers, 1990), 69-70.

79 *Ledger,* 170.

80 Emmy Lu Read ne Weed. Letters to authors, 1 January 1977, 13 January 1977, 24 January 1977.

81 *Ledger,* 171.

82 Steve Osmond. Telephone conversation with authors, 25 November 1983.

83 John J. Koblas, *Sinclair Lewis: Home at Last* (Bloomington, Minnesota: Voyageur Press, 1981), 38-41.

84 Bruccoli, *Epic Grandeur,* 77. This was not technically Fitzgerald's first sale since his pay was to be two copies of the magazine. Bruccoli, *Romantic Egoists,* 32.

85 Turnbull, *Scott Fitzgerald,* 80.

86 Bruccoli, *Epic Grandeur,* 86.

Chapter Six

The Summit
1919 to 1920

In August 1918, Scribner's rejected Fitzgerald's novel. Instead of courting Zelda as a famous novelist, he found himself using the same lines that Leslie had used on the publisher: he would soon be sent to France and die. The pitch apparently worked, but it was Fitzgerald who felt wedded to Zelda after the consummation of their affair; she continued to date other men. In late October, his regiment entrained north for embarkation to France, but to his lasting regret, the war ended.

Back at Camp Sheridan for discharge, Fitzgerald learned of the death of Father Fay in January 1919. His last formal ties to the Catholic Church dissolved, Scott turned to Zelda as a replacement for religion. When he got out of the army in February, he wired Zelda from New York City: MY ONLY HOPE AND FAITH IS THAT MY DARLING HEART WILL BE WITH ME SOON.[1] Scott secured a position with an advertising firm but was making less than he did in the army. He tried to supplement his income by writing stories at night but managed only one sale, a measly thirty dollars for a re-written *Nassau Lit* story. He continued to woo Zelda during monthly weekend trips and sent her his mother's ring,[2] but in June she broke the engagement. Fitzgerald returned to New York and started a drinking binge that ended only with the passage of prohibition on July 1.

Once he sobered up, Scott decided to return to his home-town and stake everything on a revision of his rejected novel. His

"In a house below the average
On a street above the average
In a room below the roof
With a lot above the ears"
Letter to Alida

93

Fitzgerald residence, 599 Summit Avenue. (Dave Page photo)

Above right: Speaking tube on the third floor of 599 Summit Avenue, 1983. (Dave Page photo)

parents had moved two doors west to 599 Summit, and he immediately commandeered the front room on the third floor, which gave him a bird's eye view of avenue. Outside the door of the room protrudes a speaking tube. It is easy to imagine the busy writer ringing a servants' bell, hanging just around the corner, to attract his mother, and then ordering meals via the tube. Sometimes he would skip meals entirely, relying solely upon cigarettes as stimulation for his fifteen-hour days.[3]

Scott could also lift the inside window, unlatch the screen, and crawl out to a small landing with an impressive view up and down the boulevard. Refreshed, he would come back into the room, careful not to disturb the chapter outlines pinned to the curtains. Edward and Mollie were not overly enthusiastic about their son's efforts and were upset when he turned down a job as advertising manager at Griggs Cooper & Co., a St. Paul wholesaler owned by the father of one of his friends.[4] Yet, they granted him complete privacy, launched a campaign to keep his friends away from the house, and prohibited their own curiosities from interfering in their son's business.[5]

While he worked on his novel, Fitzgerald did not touch alcohol.[6] The existence of prohibition was not the only, or even main, reason. St. Paul was the center of one of the largest bootlegging operations in the country, and plenty of liquor was available. He simply did not want anything to interfere with his concentration. Scott did not give up socializing, however. During a dinner party given by friend Sidney Stronge at the University Club, he met Yale graduate Donald Ogden Stewart, an American Telephone and Telegraph Company employee who possessed literary leanings. Stewart would later write *A Parody Outline of History* and collaborate with Fitzgerald on films in the late 1930s. Fitzgerald probably used Stewart as a model for Brimmer, a Communist organizer, in his unfinished Hollywood novel, *The Love of the Last Tycoon,* since Stewart was eventually involved in Communist politics.[7]

University club, lower bar.
(Photo by Dave Page)

Above left: Mrs. Porterfield's
Boarding House, 513
Summit Avenue, 1993.
(Photo by Dave Page)

"The first thing he said to me," Fitzgerald wrote in a 1921 *St. Paul Daily News* piece, was "Let's commit a burglary!" Stewart wanted the two of them to break the windows of the Manson home at 649 Summit, which had recently been converted into a funeral parlor. The idea of crass commercialism invading the city's most prestigious street offended Stewart, who—with the help of Fitzgerald—would become of the most popular literary humorists of his age. Stewart kept a room in Mrs. Charles Porterfield's boarding house, a spectacular Queen Anne house at 513 Summit, just a short distance from the brownstone the Fitzgeralds occupied. "While I was writing *Paradise* I saw a lot of Donald," Fitzgerald told Tony Buttitta in 1935. "He was helpful in shaping up *Paradise*."[8]

Porterfield's boarding house stands adjacent to a lavish formal garden and boasts an inviting front porch, where Fitzgerald, Stewart, and, sometimes, John DeQuedville Briggs, another boarder, discussed the state of world literature. Briggs, headmaster of Scott's old school, St. Paul Academy, was not overly impressed with Fitzgerald's work in progress, which by the end of July Scott was calling "The Education of a Personage." Briggs considered local newspaper reporter Dick Gordon to be a better writer. Still, he encouraged Fitzgerald in his endeavors.[9]

Because Mollie and Edward refused to give their son an allowance, Scott had to borrow small sums of money from Richard "Tubby" Washington, a longtime friend who lived in the same row house, when they went for Coke-and-smoke breaks at the W.A. Frost's Pharmacy in the Dakotah Building, 374 Selby, or at Rietzke's Drug just across the street in the Angus Hotel. Richard Washington was also keenly interested in writing and later became a reporter for the *St. Paul Daily News*. He would eventually own and operate the Angus, where—after the death of Edward in 1931—

St. Paul Seminary, ca. 1920.
(Courtesy of the Minnesota
Historical Society)

Mollie Fitzgerald lived off and on. (The once-elegant Angus has been restored into an office building, and W.A. Frost's continues to do a thriving business as a restaurant.).

Fitzgerald also sought literary advice from friends Katherine Tighe and Father Joe Barron, the young dean of students at St. Paul Seminary. Scott could catch an electric car of the Groveland Park Line down the entire length of Summit to the Seminary, which stands at the end of Summit on the Mississippi River. It was here the horse-drawn sleighs of Fitzgerald's youth would turn north toward the Town and Country Club.

St. Paul Seminary, 1995.
(Photo by Dave Page)

The relationship between Scott and Father Barron was a natural outgrowth of the Fitzgerald family's close ties with local Catholic organizations. Annabel McQuillan, for example, was a reliable donor to the seminary library and annually contributed the periodical *Revue Des Deux Mondes*.[10]

Father Barron, eight years older than Scott, was a Minneapolis native but grew up in the parish of St. Luke's Church, located on the corner of Lexington and Summit in St. Paul. He received a classical education from St. Thomas College, which sprawls kitty-corner from the seminary on Summit Avenue, before attending St. Paul Seminary. He was ordained in 1912 at the age of twenty-four, then studied at the Catholic University of America for Higher Studies before returning to St. Paul Seminary as a professor of logic, metaphysics and the history of philosophy in 1916.

Although Scott had drifted from the church, the two enjoyed each other's company, especially since Father Barron was himself a distinguished author, having written a widely-used textbook, *The Elements of Epistemology*.[11] He also served as the moderator for the St. Thomas Literary and Debating Society, a position that no doubt helped him in his discussions with Fitzgerald, who had not done very well academically in prep school or college but had won prizes for elocution.[12]

Father Joe Barron (left and Father P.F. O'Brien at St. Paul Seminary. (Courtesy of the St. Paul Seminary)

To his acquaintances, Father Joe was "exceptionally handsome, being nice company, and possessing a good personality and a rare gift of speech. He had a rollicking disposition and was an ardent golfer."[13] In fact, golf was Father Barron's passion, and he passed on his knowledge and skills to close associates such as Dick Lilly, president of the First National Bank of St. Paul, and Fitzgerald. Despite Fitzgerald's lack of enthusiasm for the game, Father Joe and Scott were often seen, clubs in hand, knocking balls about the lawns of the seminary.[14]

Using just seven and eight irons and a putter, the twosome would commence their game at one corner of the campus grounds and then zigzag from fairway to fairway. Trees served as hazards and provided shade during the hot August days as the duffers strolled around the seminary, chipping and putting and discussing Fitzgerald's book, which was now called, as Scott reported in a letter to Scribner's editor Maxwell Perkins, *This Side of Paradise.*

With the coming of fall, Fitzgerald's golfing and his writing ended. On September 4, he entrusted his manuscript to a friend for delivery to New York. With nothing else to do and needing the money, he decided to take a temporary job. An old friend from his Elizabethan Dramatic Club days and Princeton

Dale Street Yards, 1925.
(Courtesy of the Minnesota
Historical Society)

classmate, Laurance "Larry" Boardman secured Fitzgerald work
with his own employer, Northern Pacific Railroad. The first day at
work, Fitzgerald was ridiculed for not wearing denim. Boardman
managed to get him assigned to work by himself nailing roofing on
railroad cars. When the foreman found him sitting down to pound
the nails rather than squatting, he accused Fitzgerald of loafing.

In his short story "Forging Ahead," Fitzgerald gives us this
amusing account of his one confrontation with menial labor:

> At 6:30 the following morning, carrying his lunch, and a
> new suit of overalls that had cost four dollars, he strode self-
> consciously into the Great Northern car shops. It was like
> entering a new school, except that no one showed any inter-
> est in him or asked him if he was going out for the team. He
> punched a time clock, which affected him strangely, and
> without even an admonition from the foreman to "go in and
> win," was put to carrying boards for the top of the car.
> Twelve o'clock arrived; nothing had happened. The sun
> was blazing hot and his hands and back were sore, but no
> real events had ruffled the dull surface of the morning. The
> president's little daughter had not come by, dragged by a run-
> away horse; not even a superintendent had walked through
> the yard and singled him out with an approving eye. Un-
> dismayed, he toiled on—you couldn't expect much the first
> morning.[15]

Fitzgerald's exposure to the world of time clocks did not
last very long. On September 16, eight days before Scott's twenty-
third birthday, Scribner's sent word that it had decided to publish
his novel. "Then the postman rang, and that day I quit work and
ran along the streets, stopping automobiles to tell friends and
acquaintances about it," Fitzgerald wrote seventeen years later.
"That week the postman rang and rang, and I paid off my terrible
small debts, bought a suit, and woke every morning with a world
of ineffable toploftiness and promise."[16]

The *St. Paul Daily News,* which would give Fitzgerald more ink than any other local newspaper, ran an article on September 28, announcing over a picture of a doe-eyed Fitzgerald "His First Novel to Appear This Winter." That was Fitzgerald's hope, but Max Perkins, his editor at Scribner's, explained that a winter release was impossible.

His First Novel to Appear This Winter

F. SCOTT FITZGERALD.

From an article in the *St. Paul Daily News.* (Author's collection)

Because Scribner's had not paid him an advance on the novel, Fitzgerald knew he would have to earn something before he tried to rekindle Zelda's interest. He revised formerly rejected stories and old *Nassau Lit* plays about Ginevra and managed to sell four of them to *The Smart Set,* a magazine under the editorial direction of H.L. Mencken and George Jean Nathan. He described these literary successes in a letter he sent to the St. Paul Public Library on the last day of September:

> I am answering your letter for my mother. I haven't really got any writings yet except my book which is to be published. I've started at the magazines and sold one story to *Smart Set* (Sept. 1919 issue), one play to *Smart Set* (November 1919 issue), a poem to *Poet Lore* & that's about all. You see I am only 22, I haven't had that much chance to hit the magazines yet as the book occupied me since I left the army. I'll mail you a card when I publish anything else.[17]

Fitzgerald was actually twenty-three and the *Poet Lore* poem never appeared in print, but it was a good start for someone who just two weeks earlier had been pounding together railroad cars.

Since *Smart Set* paid a mere thirty-five to forty dollars per story, he decided to submit some stories to *Scribner's Magazine,* which paid $150 but accepted only two of his quickie efforts.[18]

St. Paul writer Grace Flandrau came to his monetary rescue in October by introducing him to a New York literary agency run by Paul Reynolds. Harold Ober, a partner in the firm, took on Fitzgerald as a client. Fearful that the Minnesota winter was hurting his health, Fitzgerald departed for New York to meet with his editor and agent. Ober had good news. He had sold the story "Nest Feathers" to George Lorimer, the editor of *The Saturday Evening Post,* for $400. Lorimer retitled the story "Head and Shoulders" and indicated he was interested in more of the same.[19] The one-two combination of Perkins and Ober would continue to service Fitzgerald's literary and financial needs throughout most of the remainder of his career.

With a little money in his pocket, Scott sneaked in a trip to Montgomery. Impressed that Fitzgerald was actually achieving what he had promised, Zelda resumed her correspondence despite rumors she was engaged to several other boys.

When Fitzgerald arrived back at 599 Summit, he set to work producing more stories. "The idea of 'The Ice Palace' grew out of a conversation with a girl out in St. Paul, Minnesota, my home," Fitzgerald wrote in a 1920 letter. As he and his date were riding home from a movie, he recalled the young lady saying "Here comes winter." Fitzgerald wondered aloud whether Swedes were not melancholy on account of the cold. Two weeks later, he was walking in a Confederate graveyard with Zelda. "She told me I could never understand how she felt about the Confederate graves, and I told her I understood so well that I could put it on paper."[20] He did, and Lorimer snapped up "The Ice Palace," which appeared in the May 1920 issue of the *Saturday Evening Post*. In it for the first time Fitzgerald examined the cultural and social differences he felt had shaped his Yankee mother and Southern father.

Encouraged by his success, Fitzgerald revised a pile of rejected stories including "Lilah Meets His Family" and "Barbara Bobs Her Hair." Lorimer took them both, and promptly changed the titles again. The first became "Myra Meets His Family," a story Fitzgerald later refused to have included in his collected stories. The second became "Bernice Bobs Her Hair"; Fitzgerald claimed this was based on a set of instructions he sent to his sister Annabel. The ten-page list was aimed at improving her social charms.[21] Although Fitzgerald labeled the story "trash" in a note to H.L. Mencken, "Bernice Bobs Her Hair" is certainly a clever, well-written story.[22] With critics, Fitzgerald would adopt the pose that the stories he wrote for the slick magazines were less literary, but he knew in his heart the skill and effort they required. Later he would write Maxwell Perkins: "I'm sick of the flabby semi-intellectual softness in which I flounder with my generation."[23]

During Christmas week, some acquaintances tried to get Fitzgerald out of his self-imposed exile. They told him he "had missed some rare doings: a well-known man-about-town had disguised himself as a camel and, with a taxi-driver as the rear half, managed to attend the wrong party." The next day Fitzgerald attempted to find out how much truth there was to the story, but no one seemed to remember the facts. "Well, I can't seem to find out exactly what happened but I'm going to write about it as if it was ten times funnier than anything you've said," Fitzgerald told his friends, then went on to create "The Camel's Back" in twenty-two consecutive hours.[24] This story, once again originally published in the *Post*, brought his first inclusion in the O. Henry Prize series and was later picked up by the movies.

Because he wrote his stories in pencil and had poor handwriting, he engaged the services of a typist. Rose Snyder Claude was employed by a law firm, located in the Commerce Building, with whom Mollie and Edward conducted occasional business. Scott was sent to her by a legal stenographer next door who did not want to accept his work because he was "very tight" in what he paid.[25] Rose admitted that Fitzgerald was not overly generous, but he did pay her on time. She claims to have transcribed "The Diamond as Big as the Ritz" and "The Ice Palace,"[26] which, Scott told her, would earn him a substantial sum. She also typed some poetry for the young writer.

"He was a very effeminate fellow," Rose recalled, "not very likable, very blond, always hard up. Not the kind to thank you, always very matter of fact."

Fitzgerald did not seem to have a high regard for Rose, either. "There's not a decent typist in town so perhaps you'll want to have this done over before you submit it," he said to his agent in a note accompanying the manuscript version of "The Diamond as Big as the Ritz."[27] He did warm up with Rose when it came to one topic: Zelda. She remembered him bringing a picture of his sweetheart to her office on one occasion. "She looked like a little flapper, had a tight-fitting cloche on her head." According to Rose, Scott was going to use the money from his short story sales to "buy a diamond" for his girl. "He wanted to be rich very badly," she summarized.

When he was not writing one afternoon, he stopped by to visit his friend Elisabeth Dean. He rambled on about his admiration for Zelda just as he had done earlier when he confided in Elisabeth about Marie Hersey and Margaret Armstrong. Scott knew his parents would not approve of his attempts to win back this "most wonderful girl," so he sought Miss Dean's approval of what he felt would be his pending engagement.[28]

That Christmas week, Fitzgerald also appeared at a dance in the large stucco turreted home of the Ordways at 523 Portland, one block off Summit.[29] The patriarch of the family, Lucius, lived in New York before coming to St. Paul and worked his way up the management of local plumbing and heating products supplier. In 1905 he bought sixty-percent interest of a sickly Two Harbors, Minnesota, abrasives firm for $25,000 and hired William L. McKnight to run the place. Minnesota Mining and Manufacturing (3M) quickly grew to become one of the nation's largest diversified production companies, and the Ordways took their place in St. Paul society as one of the city's premier families and benefactors.

IN ORDER TO ONCE AGAIN ESCAPE the Minnesota winter and the threat of tuberculosis, Scott moved to New Orleans in January and did indeed take the $600 he had earned from "The Camel's Back" to buy Zelda a platinum-and-diamond wristwatch. The diamonds seemed to do the trick, and Zelda agreed to marry Scott as soon as his novel came out. The happy suitor raced to New York, then decamped to Princeton for the release of his first novel at the end of March. Any lingering doubts Zelda may have had about attaching her wagon to Fitzgerald's rising star evaporated when Ober sold the movie rights to "Head and Shoulders" to Metro for $2,500 at the end of February and received $4,500 for the film rights to three other Fitzgerald stories.[30] When the first printing of *This Side of Paradise* sold out in twenty-four hours, it was only icing on wedding cake.[31] As promised, Zelda left Alabama with her sister Marjorie for New York to become Mrs. F. Scott Fitzgerald.

Somewhat embarrassed by Zelda's frilly Southern fashions, Scott asked his former girlfriend Marie Hersey to help Zelda select her trousseau. "[Zelda] came to New York with just ruffled organdies and little linens," Marie told an interviewer later. "She was a very smart girl, but that just wasn't the thing one wore in New York."[32]

F. Scott Fitzgerald early publicity photo for *This Side of Paradise.* (Courtesy of the Minnesota Historical Society)

On April 3, 1920, the day before Easter, dressed in a suit of midnight blue with matching hat trimmed with leather ribbons and buckles, Zelda Sayre exchanged vows with Scott Fitzgerald in the vestry of St. Patrick's Cathedral. Neither the bride's nor groom's parents were present. Zelda's sister Rosalind Smith was maid of honor and Ludlow Fowler, a Princeton classmate of Scott's, was best man. Zelda's third sister, Clothilde Palmer, arrived only to find that a nervous Fitzgerald had pushed the wedding forward, so she and her husband missed the ceremony.[33] The newly-joined couple then antagonized Rosalind by immediately leaving for the Biltmore Hotel. She felt there should have been some kind of luncheon for the wedding party.[34]

Despite the shaky start with his in-laws, Scott had reached the summit, the top of the world. He had finally won the most beautiful girl, his first novel was selling briskly, and people were taking notice, even back in hometown St. Paul. Mrs. James J. Hill informed the manager of a St. Paul bookstore that she had been searching for a good Irish Catholic writer to tackle a biography of Archbishop John Ireland for some time. Having discovered *This Side of Paradise,* she had at long last found the person for the task.

Her timing was a bit off, for Scott was drifting further and further from organized religion: "There's no use concealing the fact that my reaction . . . to apparent failure in every direction did carry me rather away from the church," he wrote to Shane Leslie about the dark days of June 1919, but he still could not understand why the "Catholic papers here seem to think [*This Side of Paradise*] was a subtle attack on the American clergy."[35]

Even had he wanted to delve into the life of a prominent Catholic clergyman, he had little time for his avocation. There were domestic obligations, parties to attend, friends to visit, and interviews to give. The *St. Paul Pioneer Press* profiled the twenty-three-year-old author just two days after the September 10, 1920, release of his first book of short stories, *Flappers and Philosophers*. Fitzgerald was assured enough to let the paper know some of the stories in the collection had been rejected their first time across an editor's desk, but vain enough to claim he had graduated from Princeton in 1917. Highlighting the importance of the relationship between Fitzgerald and his hometown, the article hinted at some mischief by boasting he had "added another St. Paul name to the list of writers who have made good, and incidentally made national rather than city property of certain rather widely held secrets concerning the doings of St. Paul society."[36]

Notes

1 Matthew Bruccoli, *Some Sort of Epic Grandeur: The Life of F. Scott Fitzgerald* (New York: Harcourt Brace Jovanovich, 1981), 96.

2 Nancy Milford, *Zelda* (New York: Harper & Row, Publishers, 1970), 42.

3 Turnbull, *Scott Fitzgerald,* 100.

4 Bruccoli, *Epic Grandeur,* 101.

5 Turnbull, *Scott Fitzgerald,* 100.

6 Bruccoli, *Epic Grandeur,* 101; Matthew Bruccoli and Jackson Bryer, eds. *F. Scott Fitzgerald: In His Own Times* (New York: Popular Library, 1971), 253.

7 Jeffrey Meyers, *Scott Fitzgerald* (New York: HarperCollins, Publishers, 1994), 329.

8 Tony Buttitta, *After the Good Gay Times* (New York: The Viking Press, Inc., 1974), 84.

9 Judy Medelman. Interview with authors. St. Paul, Minnesota, 23 April 1984.

10 St. Paul Seminary archives.

11 Obituary in *Catholic Bulletin* (St. Paul), 22 April 1939, 1.

12 *F. Scott Fitzgerald's Ledger: A Facsimile* (Washington, D.C.: Bruccoli Clark Book, 1972), 167.

13 Father Clyde Eddy. Interview with authors. St. Paul, Minnesota, 12 July 1976.

14 Msgr. Francis Gilligan. Interview with authors. St. Paul, Minnesota, 12 July 1976.

15 F. Scott Fitzgerald, *The Basil and Josephine Stories* (New York: Charles Scribner's Sons, 1973), 149.

16 F. Scott Fitzgerald, *The Crack-Up* (New York: New Directions Book, 1945), 86.

17 F. Scott Fitzgerald. Letter to Dawson Lobuston. St. Paul Public Library, 30 September 1919.

18 Bruccoli, *Epic Grandeur,* 107.

19 Henry Dan Piper, *F. Scott Fitzgerald: A Critical Portrait* (New York: Holt Rinehart and Winston, 1966), 65. Piper indicates the story was called "Variety," but that story ended up being called "Dalryrimple Goes Wrong." *As Ever, Scott Fitz,* 3,5.

20 Matthew Bruccoli and Margaret Duggan, eds., *Correspondence of F. Scott Fitzgerald* (New York: Random House, 1980), 61.

21 Bruccoli, *Epic Grandeur,* 65-66; Piper, *Scott Fitzgerald,* 67.

22 Bruccoli, *Epic Grandeur,* 147.

23 Andrew Turnbull, ed. *The Letters of F. Scott Fitzgerald* (New York: Bantam Books, 1966), 167.

24 Fitzgerald, *The Crack-Up,* 87.

25 Rose Snyder Claude. Interview with authors. St. Paul, Minnesota, 10 November 1983; Beth Kent, "Fitzgerald's Back in Town," *Grand Gazette,* August 1973, 7.

26 Although the former story was written in 1921, Scott was living in St. Paul at the time and may have hired Ms. Claude a second time.

27 Matthew Bruccoli, ed., *As Ever, Scott Fitz: Letters Between F. Scott Fitzgerald and His Literary Agent, Harold Ober, 1919-1940* (London: The Woburn Press, 1973), 28.

28 Elisabeth Dean Kennedy. Telephone conversation with authors, 15 August 1976.

29 *Ledger,* 174.

30 Piper, *Scott Fitzgerald,* 71; Bruccoli, *Correspondence,* 51.

31 Piper, *Scott Fitzgerald,* 41.

32 Kent, "Back in Town," 7.

33 Milford, *Zelda,* 62.

34 Bruccoli, *Epic Grandeur,* 131.

35 Turnbull, *Letters,* 400-401.

36 "More than Hundred Notes of Rejection Failed to Halt Scott Fitzgerald's Pen," *St. Paul Pioneer Press,* 12 September 1921, 8.

Chapter Seven

White Bear Lake
1921

AFTER A WHIRLWIND TWELVE MONTHS in the environs of New York City and another two in Europe, the Fitzgeralds discussed where their baby, due in the fall of 1921, should be born: "it seemed inappropriate to bring a baby into all that glamour and loneliness" Scott wrote as an explanation why the couple rejected staying on the East Coast.[1] Montgomery seemed a logical choice, but it was hot, and Zelda donned a swimming suit to visit one of the local pools. Pregnant women rarely went outside, let alone wore tank tops in public. Zelda was asked to leave.

After only a month in Montgomery, the Fitzgeralds decided to go "home to St. Paul."[2] Scott asked his good friend Mrs. C.O. (Xandra or Sandy) Kalman to help them get settled. She found them a home to rent in Dellwood. This exclusive community along the shores of White Bear Lake had been developed by Truman W. Ingersoll, the uncle of Scott's friend Jean Ingersoll, along with Lucius P. Ordway and William Read, father of Scott's friend Cecil.

White Bear Lake had served as a summer resort for almost seventy years by the time Scott and Zelda lived there. The first hotel opened its doors in 1853, four years before Fitzgerald's grandfather P.F. McQuillan arrived in Minnesota. It was not long before a growing St. Paul aristocracy began erecting summer cottages along the lakeshore. Choice lake lots were snapped up quickly, especially after the St. Paul and Duluth Railroad laid a rail line

"Later in the afternoon the sun went down with a riotous swirl of gold and varying blues and scarlets, and left the dry rustling night of Western summer. Dexter watched from the veranda of the Golf Club, watched the even overlap of the waters in the little wind, silver molasses under the harvest-moon. Then the moon held a finger to her lips and the lake became a clear pool, pale and quiet."

"Winter Dreams"

through the village of White Bear in 1868. Hotels continued to spring up around the lake, and by 1899, the White Bear Yacht Club was organized. After a series of temporary quarters, a club-house and nine-hole golf course opened in Dellwood in 1912. Three years later, another nine holes were added.[3]

In his short story "Winter Dreams," one of the last stories Fitzgerald wrote before leaving St. Paul for good, Fitzgerald recreated his youthful experiences at White Bear Lake. Barely disguising the setting as Black Bear Lake, the author has his hero, Dexter, visit such familiar sites as Manitou Island (called Sherry Island in the story) and the Golf Club (the White Bear Yacht Club).

The cottage Xandra found was owned by Mackey J. Thompson, a St. Paul businessman who headed a mortgage office in the Pioneer Building.[4] His summer place was situated along Highway 96 in an area referred to by many local residents as "the Hill." Scott and Zelda were fortunate that Xandra had been able to rent the Thompson home that summer. Its owner had accumulated a small fortune in farm mortgages, but after the World War I came to an end, land prices suddenly declined. Thompson was also hurt by a drop in value of his stock in Capitol Trust and Savings Bank. In need of some income, Thomas decided to lease his lake house. Mollie and Annabel traveled to Dellwood to make the final arrangements for the lease.[5]

The Thompson house, unlike the neighboring cottages, was equipped with running water and central heat. It could easily endure the onslaught of winter, and Fitzgerald expected the off-season seclusion of a summer resort town would allow him plenty of time for work, so the lease was extended through the winter months.[6] Fitzgerald was quoted in a *St. Paul Daily News* article saying "he had got tired of New York and had decided to come back to a nice quiet town to write." Indeed, he intended to produce a dozen short stories before beginning a new novel.[7] The Fitzgeralds took an immediate liking to the property and settled into their new quarters on August 15. Zelda described the setting:

> When summer came, all the people who liked summertime moved out to the huge, clear lake not far from town, and lived there in long, flat cottages surrounded with dank shrubbery and pine trees, and so covered by screened verandas that they made you think of small pieces of cheese under large meat safes.[8]

Both Scott and his mother felt the spacious home would prove to be an ideal retreat.[9] As it turns out, that was not quite the case. Fitzgerald was a celebrated author, and his return to St. Paul was reported in the *St. Paul Daily News* society pages on August 14. That same day, Scott's Princeton classmate Norris Jackson moved out to the White Bear Yacht Club for two weeks, and Elizabeth (Betty) McIntosh, the fiancée of Scott's good friend Gus Schurmeier, arrived in town to visit her future in-laws. Miss McIntosh's engagement precipitated a flurry of parties, duly chronicled in the society pages of the *St. Paul Daily News,* including a luncheon at the White Bear Yacht Club. The following Monday, Schurmeier and his fiancée attended the opening of St. Paul's theater season, an event that attracted most of Fitzgerald's friends, including Marie Hersey, Elisabeth Dean, Alida Bigelow, Xandra Kalman, and Paul Baillon. The following day, Scott's sister Annabel entertained Elisabeth with a supper held at 599 Summit, where she was still living with Mollie and Edward.[10]

Although Scott and Zelda had been to Montgomery three times since their marriage, Scott's folks had not yet met their daughter-in-law. Fitzgerald was by no means estranged from his parents, but he probably harbored no great desire to introduce Zelda to his eccentric mother and unsuccessful father. Mollie and Annabel agreed Zelda was the most beautiful woman in the world,[11] but little else exists on record about the family's feelings. Even though at one point Scott used his parents' home as a mailing address and must have made frequent trips to pick up his mail, the consensus seems to be the Fitzgerald family bored Zelda.[12] She viewed her mother-in-law as a "character"; her father-in-law as "an ineffectual cardboard figure cut out in a bygone age."[13] Although Zelda was courteous, she was not the type to mingle for the sake of convention.

Zelda was nothing if not unconventional. She wore a red jersey maternity dress to greet her husband's friends, and for the

St. Paul Daily News photo of August 28, 1921. (Author's collection)

most part did not make a good impression. "Who's your fat friend?" someone asked Xandra.[14] Looking just like a little Dutch boy's head sitting on top of a striped hot-air balloon, her photograph on the society pages of the August 28 edition of the *St. Paul Daily News* could only have added insult to insult.

Certainly the unflattering photo was not intentional, for the *St. Paul Daily News* did more to bolster Fitzgerald's reputation than any other local media source. Thomas Boyd, editor of the newspaper's "In a Corner with the Bookworm" page, mentioned Scott more than forty times during 1921 and 1922. "It is a remarkable achievement to have written one book that tickled the cognoscenti [*This Side of Paradise*]," Boyd led off his August 15 1921, column, "another that pleased the 'pleasant sheep' [*Flappers and Philosophers*], and still another that is looked forward to by the literati[*The Beautiful and Damned*], all in less than three years."[15]

The Beautiful and Damned, based on Scott and Zelda's first year of marriage in New York, was to be serialized by *Metropolitan Magazine* starting in September. Even before the Fitzgeralds had decided to return to St. Paul, Boyd had mentioned in a July 21 column that *Metropolitan* readers would be able to judge whether Fitzgerald had surpassed the triumph of his previous novel or "fallen to the level of 'The Offshore Pirate,'" a story that had appeared in the May 29, 1920, *Saturday Evening Post*. After settling in at Dellwood, Fitzgerald let Boyd see the manuscript of *The Beautiful and Damned* he was polishing for release by Scribner's the following spring. The editors at *Metropolitan* had cut 40,000 words from the original, and Boyd felt the deletions marred the serial.[16]

Fitzgerald was not particularly pleased with the editing, but at a time when *The Saturday Evening Post* was paying him $500, *Metropolitan* optioned his output at $900 each story.[17] The dozen stories he planned to finish at White Bear would give him enough of a monetary cushion, he assumed, to write another novel. Within a week of arriving at White Bear, however, Fitzgerald had fallen into the rut of promising forthcoming stories to his agent and borrowing advance money from Scribner's: "1st Story will reach you Monday absolutely," he promised his agent Harold Ober in a letter sent from Dellwood.[18] "I wrote you yesterday asking for more alms—$650.00," he reiterated to Max Perkins on September 13, 1921. "I note it here so if my other letter went astray."[19]

Unfortunately for Fitzgerald's finances, *Metropolitan* went into receivership after publishing just four of his short stories, including one he wrote at Dellwood, "Two for a Cent." Not surprisingly, it was the first of Fitzgerald's stories in which successful men make pilgrimages to their home towns. "I am not very fond of Two for a Penny [sic]," Fitzgerald later wrote Ober, "Perhaps you'd better return it to me [and] maybe I can fix it up."[20] Ironically, it became one of his most popular stories. After its April 1922 appearance in *Metropolitan Magazine*, it was included in *The Best Short Stories of 1922*, was syndicated by the Metropolitan Newspaper Service, and brought Fitzgerald's first textbook appearance, in *Short Stories for Class Reading* (1925).[21]

Although Scott hoped to use the cottage as a study, he was often interrupted by visitors. Scott's Summit Avenue neighbor Tubby Washington headed north to pay his respects. Father Joe Barron also made a pilgrimage to the Thompson home to welcome his former golf partner.

F. Scott and Zelda Fitzgerald, posed for pictures for a St. Paul newspaper at the White Bear Yacht Club, October 1921. Zelda is in her eighth month. (Courtesy of the Minnesota Historical Society)

His friends were not the only ones who responded to the cry "Fitzgerald's back in town!" Boyd, too, traveled to White Bear Lake to interview the famous novelist. Besides editing the *St. Paul Daily News* book page, he was co-owner of the Kilmarnock Bookshop at 84 East Fourth Street, which eventually became a regular stop for Fitzgerald. Although younger than Fitzgerald, Boyd had seen active service with the marines during the Germans' final push in World War I and was writing a novel based on his experiences. With encouragement from Fitzgerald, Scribner's published Boyd's *Through the Wheat* in 1923. Fitzgerald also helped Boyd's wife Peggy get her novel *The Love*

Legend published by Scribner's in 1922.

Boyd's August 28 article based on his meeting with Fitzgerald is a fascinating account of a brash young author who came down to greet the reporter in "robin's egg blue" pajamas "tightly girded in at the waist." Under the headline, "Scott Fitzgerald Here on Vacation; 'Rests' by Outlining New Novels," Boyd's interview features a large photograph of Mr. and Mrs. F. Scott Fitzgerald. Fortunately for Zelda, it is much more flattering than her picture in the same edition's society page.

Scott's favorite topic, naturally, was other writers. He discoursed on a number of the leading coeval literati from H.L. Mencken (who reminded him of a red-faced, good-natured German beer drinker) to Carl Sandburg (who "came into prominence as a poet because the great city of Chicago felt the need of a representative poet and pinned the badge on Carl because nobody else was around").

Floyd Dell, Fitzgerald told Boyd, "has reached the depth of banality in his book *Mooncalf.*" This was said despite (or perhaps to spite) the fact that both Sinclair Lewis and Wisconsin Pulitzer-winner Zona Gale thought the book—a story of a young man much like Scott's Amory in *This Side of Paradise*—one of the century's better efforts.

Fitzgerald then continued to badmouth his contemporaries: "Sherwood Anderson gets his effects in spite of his style which is very bad." When asked why he became a writer, Fitzgerald explained: "Hugh Walpole was the man who really started me writing. One day I picked up one of his books when I was riding on the train. I thought, 'If this fellow can get away with it as an author, I can too.' His book seemed to me to be as bad as possible, but I knew they sold like hot cakes. The principle thing he did was to make unessentials seem important. I dug in after that and wrote my first novel."

Scott did find some kind words for Charlie Chaplin, who he called "one of the greatest men in the world. You might as well protest against a Cunarder [ocean liner] as to protest the movies." Chaplin was having problems with critics who condemned him for his alleged leftist views. (Eventually, after a 1952 trip to Europe, he was barred from returning to America. Fitzgerald's words became reality in 1972 when Chaplin made a belated but triumphant return to the United States.)

Having recently returned from overseas himself, Scott presented his feelings on the continent:

> "Europe made very little impression on me. I rather liked London, but France and Italy represent a decaying civilization. In Italy, the house where Keats died—a close, dismal hole which looked out on a cluttered, squalid street through which diseased children ran—was to me a compendium of the affectation that people have for Italy. When Anatole France dies there will be nothing left of La Belle France."[22]

On the sensitive topic of the late upheaval, Fitzgerald conveyed to Boyd that "the war was nothing but a natural disturbance, and is eclipsed in importance by the income tax" (which had come into effect in 1913).

At the end of his piece, Boyd praised Fitzgerald for his "lucid style" and "brilliant gift of phrasing, a trick of picturization, a talent for unearthing that which lies just below the obvious." His admiration did not extend to Fitzgerald's short stories, which "almost without exception, show that there was one thing uppermost in his mind when he was writing them and that was no more nor less than $350."

In a longer version of the interview published the following year, Boyd points out he had heard rumors about Fitzgerald's possible drinking problem and admits his surprise when Scott mixed drinks with synthetic gin for Boyd and his companion but did not take any himself.[23] Boyd's sympathetic portrayal of a dedicated writer may have been an attempt to curry the popular author's favor. After all, Fitzgerald did dramatically boost both Boyd's and his wife's careers. Eventually, Boyd's Kilmarnock Bookshop would put in a hefty order for the forthcoming *The Beautiful and Damned* and organize "a sales campaign that included a promotional film to be shown in all the city's movie theaters."[24]

Most other people who crossed paths with Fitzgerald had no trouble recounting some of the escapades that would get him evicted from White Bear Lake not once, but twice; very few actually remember him doing any writing. In truth, Fitzgerald was a hard worker. Besides the immense amount of effort he put into revising *The Beautiful and Damned* while living in Dellwood, he produced two stories: "Two for a Cent," and the longer, more ambitious "The Diamond as Big as the Ritz."[25] But he was also a hard drinker, fueling himself with prodigious quantities of bootleg gin. As a consequence of an active social life and the occasional drinking spree, Fitzgerald confessed he was "having a hell of time" getting as much writing done as he wished. "I've loafed for [five] months," he wrote Perkins from Dellwood, "and I want to get to work. . . ."[26]

In the same letter, Fitzgerald talked about drinking himself to death, and he almost did. The Thompson home shared a common driveway with the neighbors, the Donahowers, and one night Fitzgerald failed to veer left. The next morning, a shocked Mr. Donahower awakened to discover an open-topped Pierce Arrow as the new centerpiece of his cherished flower garden, its famous driver fast asleep at the wheel.[27]

Boyd, who "spent many hours drinking" with Fitzgerald himself,[28] chose to ignore any public spectacles and spotlighted Fitzgerald in his weekly columns. On September 11, he quoted poet Vachel Lindsay, who had stopped in St. Paul on his way back East, as saying "your Scott Fitzgerald and his 'This Side of Paradise' book are being talked about. Don't you think that Scott Fitzgerald is a noteworthy writer?"[29] The following Sunday, Boyd wrote: "Scott Fitzgerald confides that he is anxious to read John

Rice Park with the Hotel St. Paul in the background, ca. 1920. (Courtesy of the Minnesota Historical Society)

Dos Passos' "The Three Soldiers."[30] The week after that, Fitzgerald's review of Dos Passos' book appeared on Boyd's literary page. In it, Scott contends *Three Soldiers* "is the first war book by an American that is worthy of serious notice." Then he warned that Dos Passos had almost committed the sin of imitating H.G. Wells: "Let us slay Wells, James Joyce and Anatole France," Fitzgerald concluded, "that the creation of literature may continue."[31]

Next to Fitzgerald's piece, an unsigned review of the novel *Gold Shod* makes some interesting comparisons: "Nor can I see why [novelist Newton Fuessle] should be classed with Scott Fitzgerald. He is more deadly in earnest than Mr. Fitzgerald usually is, but he has not that young St. Paul man's scintillating style."

All the publicity caused a steady stream of visitors to descend on the Thompson cottage. Boyd's own first chat with Fitzgerald was cut short by the arrival of a third visitor. Lazy afternoons of tennis, golf, and lakeshore breezes had a way of blurring into social evenings with old and new friends. "He just made a party," one White Bear Lake contemporary remembered. "If he was there, everyone had a good time."[32]

Even after the frosts of October drove away much of the summer crowd, the festivities did not end at the Thompson home. During one all-night soiree, Fitzgerald and his guests did nothing to prevent the furnace from going out. The water pipes froze, and the plush living quarters were suddenly anything but that. The owners were furious and asked the Fitzgeralds to leave after only six weeks.[33] Zelda was nine months pregnant. With limited options, the couple temporarily moved into the Hotel St. Paul.

Located in the heart of downtown at 363 St. Peter, the Hotel St. Paul did, and still does, provide guests with some of the city's finest amenities. According to the *St. Paul Daily News* society pages of October 4: "Mr. and Mrs. F. Scott Fitzgerald, who have been living in the Mackey Thompson home in Dellwood the last month, now are at the Hotel St. Paul. They will remain there for several weeks, after which they are planning to move to the home of Mrs. G.T. Schurmeier, Summit Avenue, for the winter. Mrs. Schurmeier plans to go abroad."[34]

For some reason, the Fitzgeralds did not remain nearly that long in downtown St. Paul. Within forty-eight hours, they had removed to the Commodore Hotel, located in the heart of the Hill District, Fitzgerald's old neighborhood.

Notes

1 F. Scott Fitzgerald, *The Crack-Up* (New York: New Directions Book, 1945), 29.

2 *Ibid.,* 29.

3 Carl B. Drake, et al., *The White Bear Yacht Club: Its History* (St. Paul: Bruce Publishing Co., 1961); Nancy L. Woolworth, *The White Bear Story* (White Bear Lake: N.P., 1975).

4 Mackey J. Thompson, Jr. Letter to authors, 15 November 1976; Mrs. John Farrington. Letter to authors, 30 November 1977; Mr. and Mrs. George Mairs. Telephone conversation with authors, 4 June 1977; and Harry Mackenhausen. Telephone conversation with authors, 5 June 1977. See also *St. Paul City Directories.*

5 Kathryn Boardman, "F. Scott Fitzgerald's Sister Annabell [sic] Makes Final Visit to Home City," *St. Paul Pioneer Press,* 22 August 1971, 27.

6 Mackey J. Thompson, Jr. Letter to authors, 15 November 1976.

7 "Will He Repeat?" *St. Paul Daily News,* 16 August 1921, 11.

8 Jeffrey Meyers, *Scott Fitzgerald,* (New York: HarperCollins Publishers, 1994), 76.

9 Robert Clark. Telephone conversation with authors, 18 June 1976.

10 "In Society," *The St. Paul Daily News,* 23 August 1921, 7.

11 Boardman, "Fitzgerald's Sister," 28.

12 Matthew Bruccoli, *Some Sort of Epic Grandeur: The Life of F. Scott Fitzgerald* (New York: Harcourt Brace Jovanovich, 1981), 153.

13 Sara Mayfield, *Exiles from Paradise: Zelda and Scott Fitzgerald* (New York, Delacorte Press, 1971), 73.

14 Scott Donaldson, *Fool for Love* (New York: Congdon & Weed, 1983), 69.

15 "The Literary Punchbowl," *The St. Paul Daily News,* 15 August 1921, 4.

16 "Scott Fitzgerald Here on Vacation; 'Rests' by Outlining New Novels," *St. Paul Daily News,* 28 August 1921, III, 6.

17 Matthew Bruccoli, ed., *The Price was High: The Last Uncollected Stories of F. Scott Fitzgerald* (New York: Harcourt Brace Jovanovich, 1981), 33.

18 Matthew Bruccoli, ed., *As Ever, Scott Fitz: Letters Between F. Scott*

Fitzgerald and His Literary Agent, Harold Ober, 1919-1940 (London: The Woburn Press, 1973), 25.

19 Matthew Bruccoli and Margaret Duggan, eds., *Correspondence of F. Scott Fitzgerald* (New York: Random House, 1980), 85.

20 Bruccoli, *As Ever, Scott Fitz,* 29.

21 Bruccoli, *The Price was High,* 33.

22 "Scott Fitzgerald Here on Vacation..."

23 Matthew Bruccoli and Jackson Bryer, eds., *F. Scott Fitzgerald: In His Own Time* (New York: Popular Library, 1971), 253.

24 André Levot, *F. Scott Fitzgerald* (Garden City, N.Y.: Doubleday, 1983), 112.

25 Bruccoli, *As Ever, Scott Fitz,* 27.

26 Andrew Turnbull, *The Letters of F. Scott Fitzgerald* (New York: Bantam Books, 1966), 167.

27 Mrs. Carl T. Schuneman. Telephone conversation with authors, 25 November 1977.

28 Jeffrey Meyers, *Scott Fitzgerald,* 76.

29 "In a Corner with the Bookworm," *St. Paul Daily News,* 11 September 1921, III, 6.

30 "In a Corner with the Bookworm," *St. Paul Daily News,* 18 September 1921, III, 6.

31 "In a Corner with the Bookworm," *St. Paul Daily News,* 25 September 1921, III, 6.

32 Beth Kent, "Fitzgerald's Back in Town," *Grand Gazette,* August 1973, 7.

33 Mackey J. Thompson, Jr. Letter to authors, 15 November 1976.

34 "Are at Hotel," *St. Paul Daily News,* 4 October 1921, 10.

Chapter Eight

Haunted by Time
1921 to 1922

OPENING ITS DOOR FOR THE FIRST TIME in 1921, the Commodore was a plush apartment-hotel that did not cater to the "off the street trade,"[1] but instead provided opulent temporary quarters for people between homes, certainly an apt description of the parents who were expecting their first child within the month. The Fitzgeralds had enjoyed the hospitality of, and occasionally been asked to leave, some of the finest hotels in the world—the Biltmore in New York, the Cecil in London, the Hôtel de Saint-James et d'Albany in Paris, the Royal Danieli in Venice. Still, Scott would list the Commodore as among the ten best in the world.

In the 1920s, the Commodore oozed class. Coats and ties were required; the *Wall Street Journal* and *New York Times* sat in piles on the front desk. Fitzgerald was quite comfortable in such a setting. Betty Jackson, whose brother Ted Ames was in Fitzgerald's dance class, recalled that Scott was the first in their crowd to own a tuxedo.[2] In the precious few days before winter clamped a tight lid over the Midwest, Scott and Zelda could enjoy dinner while being entertained by big bands in the rooftop garden, unfortunately destroyed by fire in 1954. When the weather turned colder, the main-floor Imperial Room provided excellent dining along with a black-and-white tiled floor for afternoon tea dances.

While Zelda waited for her child to arrive, Scott decided to rent office space downtown where he could avoid the interrup-

"In the fall of the year we got to the Commodore in St. Paul, and while leaves blew up the street we waited for our child to be born."

F. Scott and Zelda Fitzgerald
"Show Mr. and Mrs. F. to Number—"

Commodore Hotel, ca. 1943. (Author collection)

The Commodore Hotel lobby, ca. 1920. (Courtesy of the Minnesota Historical Society)

The Commodore Hotel lobby, 1994. (Photo by Dave Page)

tions that occurred in White Bear Lake. In a room with only a desk and two chairs, he worked on *The Beautiful and Damned* and cranked out "The Popular Girl."[3] Typical of many Fitzgerald stories, "The Popular Girl," published in two February 1922 issues of the *Saturday Evening Post*, has a Minnesota setting, a seventeen-year-old beauty, a country club dance, and a wealthy hero.

Warned by his friends that the *Post* would suck his talent dry, Fitzgerald nonetheless felt he needed the lucre the slick magazines afforded in order to maintain his art.[4] "I am rather discouraged," Fitzgerald wrote Ober in early 1922, "that a cheap story like *The Popular Girl* written in one week while the baby was being born brings $1500.00 + a genuinely imaginative thing into which I put three weeks real enthusiasm like *The Diamond in the Sky* [original title] brings not a thing. But by God + [*Post* editor George] Lorimer, I'm going to make a fortune yet."[5] Eventually *Smart Set* would pay $300 for "The Diamond as Big as the Ritz."

Tubby Washington, one of the few who knew the whereabouts of the downtown office, stopped by one day to borrow fifty dollars from Scott, a switch from just a few years before when Scott relied on Tubby for cigarette money. "Well, well, Tubby," Fitzgerald said as he leaned back in his chair, "now what's this all about? Got some girl knocked up in Chicago, eh?" Tubby insisted that it was nothing of the sort. Fitzgerald continued to play the man of the world, and assured Tubby he could not loan him fifty dollars, then ended by talking himself into lending forty-nine.[6] Had Fitzgerald been able to find a market, this episode might have worked its way into one of his stories since Tubby had already been the inspiration for "Dalyrimple Goes Wrong."[7]

Although Fitzgerald had found a spot where he could escape to do some writing, there was still the problem of more permanent quarters. If that were not enough, Scott and Zelda had done nothing to prepare for the arrival of their first child. It was not just Zelda who was "helpless," as Scott had reported in his *Ledger*.[8] Although both Mrs. Fitzgerald and Mrs. Sayre had sent some baby clothes, Xandra had to take the couple out to purchase diapers, a bassinet, a baby bed, and a bathtub. She arranged for the hospital room, the doctor, and round-the-clock nursing.[9] When plans to stay at the Schurmeiers' fell through, Mrs. Kalman came to the rescue. She contacted Scott to let him know he and Zelda could move into the house owned by her mother-in-law, who would be taking a trip abroad.

The Kalman house, at 626 Goodrich, had quite a history. It had originally stood on Fairmount, one block to the south. When Frank Kellogg (co-author of the Kellogg-Briand Peace Pact outlawing war, secretary of state for President Calvin Coolidge, and recipient of the 1929 Nobel Peace Prize) built his Gothic retreat in 1889, he decided to plant a formal garden beside the house in order to accommodate guests expected at a speech to be given by then-President Theodore Roosevelt. The only available space was the adjacent property.

He purchased the lot in 1905 and had the structure there moved to its present location. It was a massive undertaking, requiring a small forest of logs for rolling, a multitude of large chains, and a stable of horses and mules.[10] The house on Goodrich (a street coincidentally named after Xandra's grandfather, Judge Aaron Goodrich) was purchased in 1919 by Sarah Kalman, the mother of Xandra's husband, Oscar Kalman.[11]

In 1921, one more extraordinary event would be added to the home's history: the famous writer and his comely wife would be making their home within its walls. But the most important guest, at least to the Fitzgeralds, was yet to come.

On October 26, Scott and Zelda were blessed with the birth of their only child. The event was proclaimed on the front page of the *St. Paul Daily News*.[12] "F. Scott Fitzgerald is Father of Baby Girl," the headline read. "Mr. and Mrs. Fitzgerald, Commodore Hotel, are receiving congratulations on the birth of a daughter . . . named Scottie Fitzgerald."

Scott had wanted to name the child after himself, but fretted whether it would be proper for a daughter to be named after her father, so she was originally to be christened Patricia. Sister Margaret Burke of the Convent of the Visitation, a childhood friend of Scott's sister Annabel, suggested changing the "i" to an "e" and calling the baby girl Frances Scott Key, or Scottie,[13] although as late as 1926 Zelda would refer to her has Pat.[14]

Zelda had been taken down the hill a short distance from the Commodore to Miller Hospital for the birth. Husbands were allowed in the delivery room, and Scott rushed back and forth

> **F. SCOTT FITZGERALD IS FATHER OF BABY GIRL**
>
> Mr. and Mrs. F. Scott Fitzgerald, Commodore hotel, are receiving congratulations on the birth of a daughter, born yesterday.
>
> The baby has been named Scottie Fitzgerald.
>
> Mr. Fitzgerald is the young St. Paul novelist and short story writer.

Birth announcement in the
St. Paul Daily News.
(Author's collection)

The Miller Hospital, ca.
1920. (Courtesy of the
Minnesota Historical Society)

from the waiting room to the delivery area, taking notes. Xandra, who was sitting with Scott, quite naturally asked what he was writing. "Jesus Christ! Help! . . ." Scott replied. "Now, honestly," Xandra scolded, "what is the point?" Scott said, "Well, I might use it some day."

"That's what he always said," Xandra confessed. "He was always writing things down."[15]

Scott's *Ledger* credits Zelda with mumbling, as she awakened from the anesthesia: "Oh, God, goofo [a pet name for Fitzgerald] I'm drunk. Mark Twain. Isn't she smart—she has the hiccups. I hope it's beautiful and a fool—a beautiful little fool."[16] Anyone who has read *The Great Gatsby* will recall these words exactly parallel Fitzgerald's description of Daisy's reaction to the birth of her daughter.

Clara Kohler, a special duty nurse at Miller Hospital at the time of Scottie's birth, remembered when Scottie was born on the fifth-floor obstetrics ward. Mothers were kept on the east end; babies on the west-end nursery. According to Kohler, Mrs. Fitzgerald and the child were treated with particular care as both baby and mother had private nurses around the clock, not the usual procedure. Zelda appropriated an entire small corner of the fifth floor and seemed quite relaxed.

"At that time, mothers usually spent two weeks in the hospital," Mrs. Kohler explained. "they didn't get out of bed for a week and a half."[17]

Busybody patients paraded up and down the hall trying to peer across the buffer zone, eager for a glimpse of the mysterious newcomer who commanded all the attention. A large number of friends and acquaintances also visited. Zelda seemed to take the limelight in stride and recovered on schedule, getting exercise by "walking down the hall in gorgeous negligées."[18]

Scott came and went from the hospital daily and was extremely nervous during each visit. He was deeply worried over the welfare of the new arrival. He was not relaxed in his role as a father. With Zelda away from him for the first time since their wedding day, he could not sit alone in the house. Brooks Henderson, a patient in the hospital at the same time as Zelda, recalled the author arriving wearing his "John Held overshoes," the unclasped buckles clinking rhythmically with each step as he made his way toward her room.[19]

With his usual exuberance, Scott wired Zelda's parents: LILLIAN GISH IS IN MOURNING CONSTANCE TALMADGE IS A BACK NUMBER A SECOND MARY PICKFORD HAS ARRIVED.[20]

When Zelda moved to the rented house at 626 Goodrich with the baby, Xandra helped her procure the services of a nurse, "a human institution who was passed from family to family in St. Paul."[21] The nurse took charge and prohibited smoking near the baby and would not let anyone else hold her.[22] Norris Jackson remembered taking the short walk from his house on Grand Hill to visit the new parents. "Zelda whispered that we'd have to wait until the nurse went to bed before we could go see the baby," he recalled. "The nurse didn't want anyone else to get close to Scottie."[23]

In early November, Aunt Annabel McQuillan put Scott, his sister Annabel, the nurse, and Scottie in her electric car and motored to the Convent of the Visitation at Fairmount and Grotto for the baptism of the baby. Zelda did not attend, so Scott's sister was to stand in her place. True to form, the nurse would not let

The Fitzgerald house, 626 Goodrich. (Photo by Dave Page)

her handle the baby, so the priest said to put her hand on Scottie and that would have to do.[24]

In December, little Scottie made her first appearance in the society pages of the local papers. The *St. Paul Pioneer Press* ran a Christmas story entitled "Santa Makes First Visit to Many Society Babies." Beside a large photograph of the baby, the story mentioned "December 26 will be an important date in the life of little Miss Scotty Fitzgerald, for she will be two months old on that day. Scotty is the daughter of the novelist, F. Scott Fitzgerald, and Mrs. Fitzgerald. The Fitzgeralds are spending the winter in St. Paul having leased Mrs. Arnold Kalman's house at 626 Goodrich avenue."[25]

As THE WEATHER TURNED COLDER, Scott and Zelda became restless. "St. Paul is dull as hell," Scott wrote to his friend Edmund Wilson in November.[26] In January, he complained to Wilson again in almost the same terms: "I'm bored as hell out here."[27]

Occasional breaks in the routine included dances at the University Club and visits to friends. May Maginnis Murphy remembered one Sunday afternoon when the Fitzgeralds brought Scottie to her parents' home at 661 Lincoln. Zelda carried Scottie, "a wee thing," in a basket. "They were a fascinating couple," she reminisced, "outgoing, had their own way of living, very Bohemian. Zelda was a knockout with gorgeous hair."

Mrs. Murphy's brother-in-law, J. Hyatt Downing, was living at the house. The author of *A Prayer for Tomorrow*, he was one of the regulars at the Kilmarnock Bookstore. "I was not very talkative then," Mrs. Murphy admitted, "and their conversations were way above me."[28]

Scott continued walking to his office for writing sessions. He reported it was a twenty-minute walk, but on particularly cold days he could take the trolley, which he could intercept two blocks from the house. Jean Putnam, who lived across the street from the Fitzgeralds, used to tell Mary Murphy, who bought 626 Goodrich in 1970, stories about Fitzgerald. Mrs. Putnam claimed the office was located in the St. Paul Building, still presiding at the corner of Fifth and Wabasha.[29] Other neighbors and acquaintances disagree with Mrs. Putnam on the writing studio's exact whereabouts.

In any event, Fitzgerald often found himself heading in the direction of the Guardian Building at Fourth and Minnesota in the early dusk of winter afternoons. Once there, he would enter the Kilmarnock Bookshop, stroll through the cluttered aisles of the salesroom, enter a rear chamber, and settle into one of the soft chairs near a fire. The Boyds were always on hand to greet weary visitors and partake in discussions about literature, music, or art.

Father Barron occasionally dropped by for a chat, and sometimes distinguished guests, including author Joseph Hergesheimer, made pilgrimages to the bibliophiles' delight.

Hergesheimer's fame had crested with his latest novel, *Cytherea*, and he was still glowing with its success when he stopped in St. Paul on his way back East from Hollywood where he had scored another hit with his scenario for *Tol'able David.* Fitzgerald had earlier confessed to Boyd that he did not "care much for Joseph Hergesheimer."[30] He may have been jealous of the older author's financial success, but he could have also held a grudge against one of Hergesheimer's friends, Frances Newman, who had accused him of plagiarizing Compton Mackenzie's *Sinister Street* in *This Side of Paradise.* Princeton classmate Edmund Wilson had called Fitzgerald's first novel "an exquisite burlesque of Compton Mackenzie" with no fallout, but Newman's review drew Scott's ire. He wrote her an angry letter in reply and she called him a small, spoiled boy.[31] He was still sore from Newman's retort when he met her friend Hergesheimer.

Front hall of the 626 Goodrich house, 1982. A photo of F. Scott Fitzgerald remained in the front hall through several owners. (Photo by Dave Page)

Over a few glasses of wine, Scott discovered his rival to be a hardworking artist, and invited the novelist home to meet Zelda. Several versions exist of the dinner conversation, but the thrust of the conversation centered on Fitzgerald's complaint that writing was a thankless job. Hergesheimer, although he had written for fourteen years without selling a book, disagreed but then went on to recount his hardships in the Appalachian mountains. "But, at least," countered Zelda, "you didn't have to live in St. Paul on the edge of the Arctic Circle."[32]

The foul weather was not the only thing on Zelda's mind. Scott had started work on a play he hoped would be his financial salvation. "I am writing an awfully funny play that's going to make me rich forever," he wrote Perkins. "I'm so damned tire of the feeling that I'm living up to my income."[33] When concentrating on his work, Scott had a tendency to ignore his wife. With few friends and a distaste for St. Paul's form of raised-eyebrow Victorianism she felt should have died decades earlier, Zelda lashed out at her husband, shielding none of the contempt she held for her new environment.

Attempting to placate his unhappy wife, Scott decided to round up the old gang for a reunion bobsled ride. Benjamin Griggs remembered Scott assembled as many friends as he could for a New Year's Eve party. They rendezvoused at the University Club, anxiously awaiting the arrival of the horse-drawn wagon. After loading onto the sleighs, the group headed west on Summit then turned south through Highland Park, considered "out in the country" at this time.[34] Zelda seemed to be enjoying the winter frolic, for she was continually pushing people off the sleigh on the way to Fort Snelling. While most of the merry makers thought Zelda was having a good time, others thought she acted a bit "tipsy."[35]

Quite unusually, the revelers did not stop to warm themselves anywhere on the lengthy round trip. By the time the party turned around at Fort Snelling for the long haul back, everyone's toes and fingers were feeling the effects of the prolonged cold. Yet, the leg home passed swiftly, and the relieved riders with their red noses were soon back at the University Club warming their outsides by the fire and their insides with supper.[36]

As much as Zelda seemed to enjoy the ride, she found herself living out her husband's story "The Ice Palace":

> It was a particularly cold night. A sudden thaw had nearly cleaned the streets the day before, but now they were traversed again with a powdery wraith of loose snow that traveled in wavy lines before the feet of the wind, and filled the lower air with a fine-particuled mist. There was no sky—only a dark, ominous tent that draped in the tops of the streets and was in reality a vast approaching army of snowflakes—while over it all, chilling away the comfort form the brown-and-green glow of lighted windows and muffling the steady trot of the horse pulling their sleigh, interminably washed the north wind. It was a dismal town after all, she thought—dismal.[37]

The month after Zelda got out of Miller hospital, 18.1 inches of snow fell in St. Paul, and the sun poked through the clouds only five times.[38] Even worse, there were four dismal months of winter to go. "We are both simply mad to get back to New York," she wrote to Scott's best man, Ludlow Fowler. "This damned place is 18 below zero."[39] Even though Scott agreed in principle, many times discussions concerning their living situation turned into roaring fights, and the neighbors were treated to these verbal fireworks. "Arguments were always violent," one young neighbor remembered. "They never held back; they just screamed at one another."[40]

Although Fitzgerald might voluntarily become a public spectacle, he rarely gave speeches. For a change of pace, he spoke before the Women's City Club of St. Paul on December 1. The title of his speech was "South America," but that was meant to be humorous, as was much of the rest of his lecture. He denied he invented bobbed knees, then went on to speak about his own writing: "The flapper is interested in shocking people. None of my heroines ever cared enough about people to know whether they were shocking them or not. . . . I cannot understand why, whenever the word flapper is mentioned, my name should be dragged headlong into the conversation. I know nothing about flappers."[41]

Once again, it seems Scott had seen into the future. St. Paul newspapers, with only a few exceptions, treated him as society sensation or an expert on the flapper. "Fitzgerald Condemns St. Paul Flappers" read one headline in 1922. The next year "What a 'Flapper Novelist' Thinks of His Wife," appeared in the local newsstands. Ten years later, it was still "'Kids of Ex-Flappers Have Pretty Sorry Treatment,' F. Scott Fitzgerald Asserts."

TO BLOW SOME LIFE BACK into the arctic wastes of St. Paul, Scott and Zelda and a few friends organized a "bad luck ball" on Friday, January 13, 1922. The Fitzgeralds "were always thinking up perfectly killing things to do," Xandra Kalman said, "entertaining stunts which were so gay that one wanted to be in on them."[42] They hung black crepe at the University Club and passed out copies of *The St. Paul Daily Dirge* whose banner headline read "Cotillion is Sad Failure." The paper carried stories about fist fights among St. Paul figureheads and wives forced to sell used clothes to support their millionaire husbands. The *Pioneer Press* ran a piece the following Sunday, calling the party "one of the merriest affairs of the season."[43] The sub-heading of the article read: "F. Scott Fitzgerald Is Editor and News Hound for Saffron-Tinted Journal Issued as Feature of Sad-Toned, Bad Luck Ball." The real *St. Paul Daily News* followed up with a story of its own entitled "F. Scott Hides Following Bow of 'The Dirge,'" a tongue-in-cheek article that claimed the author was holed up in his Goodrich Avenue home not taking any visitors.[44]

The Fitzgeralds may have indeed been avoiding society, but the reason was that both of them were ill, possibly from too much alcohol.[45] Zelda's drinking and smoking were duly noted and certainly weighed against her in polite society. Someone knew someone who saw Zelda throw liquor bottles from automobiles.[46] Others caught her smoking at the back of street cars. She danced too suggestively.[47] "I think Zelda was Scott's downfall," one unidentified acquaintance told an interviewer years later. "She just liked parties too much." Another put it just as bluntly, "Zelda? No. I didn't like her—she wasn't the type I care about. I like quiet people."[48] Ironically, others complained she uninvited people Scott had earlier asked over for drinks,[49] and put an end to several noisy celebrations at the house by warning they would wake the baby.[50]

Most, if not all, these stories are probably true. Mrs. Kalman, one of Zelda's few friends in St. Paul, admitted "there weren't many people whom [Zelda] liked. I won't say she was rude, but she made it quite clear. If she didn't like someone or if she disapproved of them, then she set out to be as impossible as she could be."[51]

Even Father Barron, who respected Zelda, did not escape her cynicism. She once told the young priest that she felt most people—especially writers—took money too seriously. Father Barron countered: "All right, Zelda—supposing Scott's stuff stopped selling and you saw a dress that you wanted more than anything in the world, and to get it you'd have to spend your last hundred dollars. What would you do?"

"I'd buy the dress," Zelda answered

Barron told her she was just posing, she countered, and the argument went on until Barron declared she couldn't be that tough; nothing in her life conditioned her for it. All the while, Scott listened in silence, holding a drink and smiling.[52]

It is quite understandable that Scott's loyal St. Paul friends would blame any problems in his marital relationship on his wife—the outsider—yet some of those closest to the Fitzgeralds recognized the two-way nature of their destructive relationship. "Zelda and Scott burned each other out, ruined each other's lives," Betty Jackson observed.[53] About the only consensus St. Paul society reached about Zelda was that she was extremely attractive, possessed of sharp features, a petite figure, a hypnotic voice, sparkling eyes, and blonde, beautiful hair. Matched with Scott's soft blue irises, almost feminine facial features and immaculate taste in clothes, the Fitzgeralds made a strikingly handsome couple.

Xandra Kalman was one of the few people in St. Paul who recognized Zelda as an extremely gifted person with few outlets for her talent. "Zelda was a very positive person," she explained in a 1975 interview, "knew exactly what she wanted and was extremely intelligent." Xandra actually thought Zelda was a better writer than her husband because he had no imagination: "Scott's letters weren't particularly interesting."[54]

To be fair, Scott also recognized the brilliance of his wife and asked her opinion about his work. Zelda was the one who told him to cut the moralizing at the end of *The Beautiful and Damned*, and after Perkins agreed, Scott reworked the conclusion to its present form.

In March, Thomas Boyd ran a series of articles on Fitzgerald that were both perceptive and proselytical. The editor of the *St. Paul Daily News* literary page noted that when he first came to St. Paul, acquaintances of Fitzgerald told him Scott was "an awful snob" and reported he was sequestered in a New York apartment drinking $10,000 worth of liquor.[55] Having previously noted that Fitzgerald did not drink the gin he and a friend brought to White Bear Lake from St. Paul, Boyd went on to say that most of Scott's friends were willing to make the ten-mile drive to White Bear Lake "to warm themselves in the warm rays thrown off by [Fitzgerald's] glory."[56] Boyd agrees that Fitzgerald is an inspiration, and says "To be with him for an hour is to have the blood in one's veins thawed and made fluent."

Boyd admits he was apprehensive about Scott's reaction to his first interview published the previous August and anxious to form a friendship. He praises Fitzgerald's way with words ("Figures of speech swiftly flap their wings toward the open door of his mind"[57]) and quotes the author's disparagement of alcohol: "For me, narcotics are deadening to work. I can understand any one drinking coffee to get a stimulating effect, but whiskey—oh, no."

The dean of St. Paul literary society, Charles Flandrau, whose wife had helped Fitzgerald find a literary agent, was not so kind. In a piece entitled "Modernity—What Flandrau Heard in a Book Shop," Flandrau wrote about a flapper ordering "six copies of Fitzgerald's 'The Boozeful and Damned.'"[58] James Gray, critic for the *St. Paul Dispatch*, could never convince Flandrau that Fitzgerald's writing was more than "post-graduate flapperism."[59]

Scott and Zelda's escape to New York City ostensibly to celebrate the release of *The Beautiful and Damned* turned out much closer to Flandrau's teasing than Boyd's tribute. The peripatetic couple left Scottie in care of the nurse and headed East at the end of March, a time of year Midwesterners call spring, but which is really only a break between the chill and snow of winter and the humidity and mosquitoes of summer: "Without elation, without an interval of moist glory," Fitzgerald explained in "Winter Dreams," "the cold was gone."[60]

Dexter's feelings about the Wasteland-like quality of April foreshadowed once again the Fitzgeralds' own experience in New York that spring. Zelda had an abortion; Scott drank. Zelda moped about Scott's attentions to Dorothy Parker, the Algonquin wit he met through publisher Horace Liveright; Scott drank some more.[61] "My original plan was to contrive to have long discourses with you," he later wrote Edmund Wilson, "but that interminable party began and I couldn't seem to get sober enough to tolerate being sober. In fact the whole trip was largely a failure."[62]

Back home in St. Paul, the famous couple continued to attract attention. One former neighbor recalled groups of the curious mulling in the shadows in front of the Fitzgerald residence on

The front windows of the 626 Goodrich house, 1982. (Photo by Dave Page)

Goodrich. A sampling of these gawkers would stroll casually by the house in hopes of catching a glimpse of the author, but there were also aggressive types who militantly paraded outside, standing their ground at the bottom of the front steps, unabashed by their own obvious behavior.[63]

Children were especially attracted to Fitzgerald, and he went out of his way—most of the time—to be kind to them. Mrs. Putnam, who lived across the street from the Fitzgeralds, loved to talk about Fitzgerald with a later owner of the Goodrich residence, Mary Alice Murphy. She would tell Mrs. Murphy that Scott came outside in a necktie with his sleeves rolled up. "Most men wouldn't come out without a jacket, let along their sleeves rolled up."[64]

Ruth Blake had similar memories of her famous next-door neighbor. "He was a delightful person," she recalled. "He used to come out on the step and sit with us, and we kids all held him in awe. He was very friendly and talkative, and he always promised that he would put us all in a story." The disappointment in her voice showed when she concluded, "But he never did."[65]

Ruth would ride her pogo stick back and forth on the sidewalk and sometimes sneak up to the house to press her face, along with other neighborhood pixies, against the windows. What they would have seen was a setting very similar to Act I of Fitzgerald's play, originally titled "Gabriel's Trombone," but published as *The Vegetable.* One of the later owners of the house on Goodrich admitted, just like Fitzgerald's description in the play, the front windows were "an awful bother to raise."[66] Likewise, there were built-in bookcases in the living room of Goodrich Avenue home and in the living room of Jerry Frost's house in the play.

When no one expressed an interest in producing the play in early 1922, Fitzgerald continued to polish the second act.

Fitzgerald's most memorable description of the house at 626 Goodrich, or one just like it, occurred in "Author's House." In it, the author sees children playing through his front window, then takes his guest upstairs to his bedroom where he writes "when there are too many children around."

He invites the guest further up in the house. "Up?" the guest questions. "Up to the attic," the author replies. The two go up to the attic, and the author invites the guest to go higher still. "Where?" wonders the guest. "Up to the cupola—the turret, the watch-tower, whatever you want to call it. I'll lead the way."

"It is small up there," Fitzgerald writes, "and full of baked silent heat until the author opens two of the glass windows that surround it and the twilight wind blows through. As far as your eye can see there is a river winding between green lawns and trees and purple buildings and red slums blended in by a merciful dusk."[67] The house on Goodrich also has a tower with little glass windows from which a bold explorer could catch glimpses of the Mississippi River and downtown St. Paul.

If the neighborhood children became too much of a bother, Fitzgerald would go outside and throw nickels at them in an attempt to bribe them away.[68] This action probably encouraged a

The third floor of the 626 Goodrich home. The tower had a bathroom in 1983. (Photo by Dave Page)

F. Scott Fitzgerald in the *St. Paul Daily News*. (Author's collection)

return to the scene of the crime for five more cents' worth of candy and two more cents' worth of the promise of literary immortality.

Scott wrote only one short story during the winter and spring of 1922, "The Curious Case of Benjamin Button." It traces the life of a man who is born old and grows young. Ober had trouble placing this fanciful story, just as he had trouble placing "The Diamond as Big and the Sky," but eventually sold it to *Collier's* for $1,000. Scott was not relaxing, however, he kept busy by revising *The Vegetable* and writing a musical comedy for the St. Paul Junior League called *The Flappers of Midnight*, in which both he and Zelda had roles. A preview of the show in the April 2 *Daily News* hinted that Fitzgerald had "composed what is reported to be one of the cleverest extravangzas [sic] that any author has ever written for any chapter of the Junior league."[69]

Junior League play written by F. Scott Fitzgerald, October 1921. Fitzgerald, (second from right) plays a priest in a mock wedding. (Courtesy of the Minnesota Historical Society)

The day before the Junior League play opened on April 17, the *Daily News* reprinted on its front page an interview Fitzgerald had given in New York. In it, he lambasted the Midwestern woman: "She is unattractive, selfish, snobbish, egotistical, utterly graceless, talks with an ugly accent and in her heart knows that she would feel more at home in a kitchen than in a ballroom."[70] Fitzgerald did admit Midwestern women enjoyed good health, but added Southern women were the most attractive in America.

Besides giving questionable interviews, Fitzgerald had met David Selznick in New York and agreed to write a movie synopsis for him. In April he mailed 1,500 words to Selznick, but the producer turned the idea down. Zelda had better luck with an assignment she received in New York. Burton Rascoe asked her to review *The Beautiful and Damned* for the *New York Tribune.* Writing under her maiden name, Zelda quickly produced a witty commentary, published April 2, 1922, suggesting readers should purchase the book for "aesthetic reasons: first, because I know where there is the cutest cloth-of-gold dress for only three hundred dollars. . . ." She went on to suggest her "Friend Husband's Latest" may have included a bit of her work:

> It seems to me that on one page I recognized a portion of an old diary of mine which mysteriously disappeared shortly after my marriage, and also scraps of a letter which, though considerably edited, sound to me vaguely familiar. In fact, Mr. Fitzgerald—I believe that is how he spells his name—seems to believe that plagiarism begins at home.

Zelda's piece, her first published work since she left high school, ends in an equally humorous vein. She notes that Scott has written a tragedy unequaled by any work of Thomas Hardy—for Gloria, with thirty million to spend, buys an ordinary sable coat instead of a Tatar sable.[71]

Zelda and Scottie. (*St. Paul Daily News* photo)

Shortly afterward, *Metropolitan Magazine* published an essay by Zelda called the "Eulogy on the Flapper."[72] For the year 1922, Scott kept a separate account for Zelda's earnings, a respectable $815.[73] At the same time Zelda was enjoying a modicum of success, Scott mailed his agent a 25,000-word serial based on a car trip to Montgomery in 1920. The *Post* rejected it. "The Cruise of the Rolling Junk" took Ober two years to sell and brought only $300.[74]

In May, Scott purchased a car and occasionally would take his father to purchase cigars at Wesley St. Clair's Grotto Pharmacy at 740 Grand. A St. Paul resident, who as a boy served as a clerk at the drugstore, recalled Scott driving up with his father in a new Buick touring car. It was a gorgeous automobile, red with a tan top, and its owner took great pride in its appearance. When the young writer exited the fancy transportation with his bearded Victorian father, the pair attracted attention.

The two men entered the drugstore, and as usual, the elder Fitzgerald hurried to the tobacco counter. His favorite brand was the Tom Moore Cigar, and Scott offered to buy a box for his father. Edward shook his head and whispered, "Forget it. You have a wife and child to support." Edward paid for the cigars himself, and the two left the store and drove away down Grand Avenue.[75]

AS THE WEATHER TURNED WARMER, the Fitzgeralds left their home on Goodrich and returned to White Bear Lake for the summer, this time finding lodging at the White Bear Yacht Club. Zelda swam and golfed while Scott worked on a second book of stories eventually published as *Tales of the Jazz Age*. Sales of *The Beautiful and Damned* were not as high as Scott had anticipated, and soon he was in need of cash. Outlook Photoplays seemed to come to the rescue by taking an interest in *This Side of Paradise* and even considered Scott and Zelda for the lead roles, but the deal fell through when Outlook failed to pay the $3,000 option money.[76]

Although Scott made noises about beginning another novel, the project did not get past the notion stage. He wrote Perkins to say that when he completed organizing the book of stories, "I may start my novel and I may not. Its locale will be the middle west and New York of 1885 I think."[77] A year would go by before Fitzgerald began serious work on *The Great Gatsby*, but the seeds would be planted the last few months he spent in Minnesota.

No writing was possible among the distractions of the summer resort. Weekly or more frequent dances were held at the club, and—since Scottie's nurse had followed them to their new quarters—the Fitzgeralds were seldom absent. One woman who attended yacht club parties with the Fitzgeralds recalled them both being handsome, particularly Scott, whom she considered extremely attractive. During one of the gala affairs, Zelda drank to excess, passed out, and was carried upstairs to bed. The dance continued without her, and Scott was soon mingling with the celebrants.[78]

Visitors continued to besiege the popular author, and Fitzgerald obliged them in the couple's suite or the club's smaller rooms. Norris Jackson remembered one time when he and Princeton classmate Hank Ford were out golfing and stopped by for a chat. The phone rang and Scott went to answer it. "He came back a few minutes later and said, 'Aw, shucks, I've got to go get some gin and lemons because Sinclair Lewis is coming over,'" Norris said. The group moved to a larger room and the famous fellow Minnesotan arrived. Soon Mr. Jackson and his friend excused themselves since the talk had turned to literature, a topic which Norris admitted tended to bore him.[79]

Lewis did not particularly care for the younger author's work. Instead, he would prefer Ernest Hemingway and, later, John Steinbeck. The Noble prize winner was especially fond of playwright Eugene O'Neill and considered writing plays himself. But, like Fitzgerald, he did not possess the necessary tools of a dramatist.

Lewis refused to discuss Fitzgerald or his work publicly, even when pressed. The most one could get out of him was that he was proud of this Minnesota son who was causing such a sensation.[80] Some were not fooled by the bonhomie and insisted the two writers did not like each other.[81] Minnesota novelist Margaret Culkin Banning, an acquaintance of the two men, cursed both their houses. "Both Lewis and Fitzgerald had dreadful personalities," she quipped. "The difference was that Fitzgerald could write."[82]

One gathering followed another, and often the festivities would continue into the night. Since most of the club members desired peace and quiet, club officials made a decision to ask the Fitzgeralds to leave the last week of August.[83] In a replay of the previous summer, the couple packed their things and returned to the Commodore Hotel.

While making plans to vacate St. Paul in favor of New York, Scott wrote one of his best stories, "Winter Dreams," what Matthew Bruccoli calls the "most important of the Gatsby cluster stories" and "virtually a preview of *The Great Gatsby*."[84] In fact, Fitzgerald lifted the description of Judy Jones' house from the magazine story and dropped it into his novel for Daisy Fay's home.

One myth that persists about the Commodore is that Fitzgerald drank in its famous art deco Mirror Bar. Created by a Hollywood set designer in 1936, the bar still has its low tables, black and white decor, mirrored walls and amber lights that reflect off gold-leafed domes, but Fitzgerald, who never returned to St. Paul after 1922, could not have stepped foot in it.

That is not to say that Fitzgerald did not imbibe at the Commodore. He did, but in a much less public setting than the

Commodore Hotel's Imperial Room. Scott danced here with his friends. (1994 Photo by Dave Page)

Mirror Bar. Although Scott's stories may have given literary shape to the Roaring Twenties, its parameters were set by Prohibition. The Volstead Act—named after the United States Representative from Minnesota, Andrew Volstead, whose offices were on the fifth floor of the nearby Landmark Center—had been the law of the nation for several years. It did not specifically prohibit the consumption of alcohol, just its sale, manufacture, and transportation. Because St. Paul was a major rail center and Minnesota provided hundreds of miles of border wilderness over which to smuggle liquor from Canada, Minnesota's capital became one of the leading providers of illicit booze to a thirsty country. ". . . you could buy it in any drugstore," recalled St. Paul crime reporter Nate Bomberg,[85] a line used by Fitzgerald in *The Great Gatsby* when Tom Buchannan hints at Gatsby's shady past by saying "You can buy anything at a drug store nowadays."[86]

As a nod at the law, decorum required the Commodore's lounge to be located in the Commodore's basement. "We didn't call it a 'speakeasy' then," remembered Mrs. C.J. Claude, the secretary who typed Fitzgerald's stories. "You had to know someone to get in. I didn't know anyone, but my husband did."[87]

Dan Runyon, a former manger of the present bar, explained the admission process further. "There were two entrances to the basement during those times. The one from the lobby of the hotel led right into the lounge. It's been tiled over since. The entrance outside the hotel required knocking at a door which had a sliding partition. If you were recognized, you were let into a foyer where you waited to be admitted to the main lounge."[88]

Scott and Zelda once again did not have much time to enjoy the hotel's hospitality, for in early September they turned their backs on St. Paul for the last time. Arriving in New York in the middle of a heat wave, they rented a suffocating suite at the Plaza Hotel. A few days later, rainstorms flooded the city. Biographer André, LeVot has noted the similarities to *Gatsby*:

> These meteorological details would be gratuitous had they not been converted into drama in the final chapters of Gatsby. The scene at the Plaza in which Daisy rejects Gatsby . . . is described as taking place in September 1922, on "almost the last, certainly the warmest [day] of the summer." Gatsby is murdered a few days later and he is buried in a downpour six days after his defeat. The coincidence is really too strong to be accidental; this was Fitzgerald's imagination distilling the effective essence from these climatic vagaries.[89]

After Scott and Zelda found a house in Great Neck, Zelda returned to St. Paul for the baby, who had been left with the nurse. Mother and daughter rejoined Scott a few days later. F. Scott Fitzgerald would come to St. Paul no more; neither would Zelda.

Notes

1 Robert L. Roedocker, "The Commodore Revisited," *The Grand Gazette,* Sept.-Oct. 1973, 1.

2 Betty Ames Jackson. Interview with authors. St. Paul, Minnesota, 9 April 1983.

3 Arthur Mizener, *The Far Side of Paradise: A Biography of F. Scott Fitzgerald* (Boston: Houghton Mifflin Company, 1951), 134.

4 Jeffrey Meyers, *Scott Fitzgerald* (New York: HarperCollins Publishers, 1994), 80.

5 Matthew Bruccoli, ed., *As Ever, Scott-Fitz: Letters Between F. Scott Fitzgerald and His Literary Agent, Harold Ober, 1919-1940* (London: The Woburn Press, 1973), 36.

6 Mizener, *Paradise,* 136.

7 *Ibid.*

8 *F. Scott Fitzgerald's Ledger: A Facsimile* (Washington, D.C.: A Bruccoli Clark Book, 1972), 176.

9 Sara Mayfield, *Exiles from Paradise: Zelda and Scott Fitzgerald* (New York: Delacorte Press, 1971), 73.

10 Mary Alice Murphy. Interview with authors. River Falls, Wisconsin, 23 April 1984; Peter B. Phelps. Telephone conversation with authors, 23 April 1984; George Muschamp, Interview with authors. St. Paul, Minnesota, 24 April 1984.

11 Xandra Kalman. Letter to authors, 24 April 1984; Donald Empson, *The Street Where You Live* (St. Paul: Witsend Press, 1975), 59.

12 "F. Scott Fitzgerald is Father of Baby Girl," *St. Paul Daily News,* 27 October 1921, 1.

13 Theresa Kump, "Fitzgerald's St. Paul: The Romantic Egoist at Home," *Little Bit,* April 1975, 11.

14 Nancy Milford, *Zelda* (New York: Harper & Row, 1970), 84.

15 Alexandra Kalman. Interview with Lloyd Hackl. St. Paul, Minnesota, 1975. Tape recording, Minnesota Historical Society, St. Paul, Minnesota.

16 *Ledger,* 176.

17 Clara Kohler. Interview with authors, St. Paul, Minnesota, 12 November 1983.

18 *Ibid.*

19 Brooks Henderson. Interview with authors. St. Paul, Minnesota, 2 August 1976. John Held was a popular cartoonist of that era whose characters he often outfitted with buckled footgear which became known as "John Held overshoes," although the designers never used that title. Fitzgerald himself described his clinking buckles echoing down an earlier hall—St. John's Episcopal Church. Held actually did the cover for Fitzgerald's book of short stories *Flappers and Philosophers,* and forever after, Held's cartoon girls and Fitzgerald's fictional flappers were linked in the public's mind.

20 Andrew Turnbull, *Scott Fitzgerald* (New York: Charles Scribner's

Sons, 1962), 127.

21 Kathryn Boardman, "F. Scott Fitzgerald's Sister Annabell [sic] Makes Final Visit to Home City," *St. Paul Pioneer Press,* 22 August 1971, 28.

22 *Ibid.*

23 Norris Jackson, Interview with authors. St. Paul, Minnesota, 11 November 1982.

24 Boardman, "Fitzgerald's Sister," 28.

25 Elizabeth Forman, "Santa Makes First Visit to Many Society Babies," *St. Paul Pioneer Press,* 25 December 1921, III, 1.

26 Andrew Turnbull, ed., *The Letters of F. Scott Fitzgerald* (New York: Dell Publishing Co, Inc., 1966), 353.

27 Turnbull, *Letters,* 354.

28 May Maginnis Murphy. Telephone conversation with authors, 9 November 1983.

29 Mary Alice Murphy. Interview with authors. St. Paul, Minnesota, 23 April 1984.

30 "Scott Fitzgerald Here on Vacation; 'Rests' by Outlining New Novels," *St. Paul Daily News,* 28 August 1921, III, 6.

31 Mayfield, *Exiles,* 76-77.

32 *Ibid.,* 77.

33 John Kuehl and Jackson Bryer, eds., *Dear Scott/Dear Max* (New York: Charles Scribner's Sons, 1971), 271.

34 Benjamin Griggs. Letter to authors, 28 March 1984.

35 Elizabeth Griggs Clark. Letter to Virginia Martin, August 1978.

36 Benjamin Griggs. Interview with authors. St. Paul, Minnesota, 27 March 1984.

37 Malcolm Cowley, *The Stories, of F. Scott Fitzgerald* (New York: Charles Scribner's Sons, 1951), 76-77.

38 "18 Inches of Snow and Only Five Clear Days was November Record," *The St. Paul Daily News,* 2 December 1921, 1.

39 André LeVot, *F. Scott Fitzgerald* (Garden City, N.Y.: Doubleday, 1983), 113.

40 Ruth Blake. Interview with authors. St. Paul, Minnesota, 25 May 1984.

41 "Scott Fitzgerald Speaks at Home," *St. Paul Daily News,* 4 December 1921, II, 6.

42 LeVot, *Scott Fitzgerald,* 112.

43 "The Daily Dirge Bemoans Failure of Cotillion on Double Jonah Day," *St. Paul Pioneer Press,* 15 January 1922, III, 1.

44 Matthew Bruccoli, et al., eds., *The Romantic Egoist* (New York: Charles Scribner's Sons, 1974), 88.

45 *Ledger,* 176.

46 Bonnie Lake, "Half A Century Later...Fitzgerald legends endure,"

Sun Illustrated, 9 April 1974, 8.

47 Mizener, *Paradise,* 150.

48 Beth Kent, "Fitzgerald's Back in Town," *Grand Gazette,* August 1973, 7.

49 Mizener, *Paradise,* 151.

50 Mayfield, *Exiles,* 78.

51 Levot, *Scott Fitzgerald,* 112.

52 Turnbull, *Scott Fitzgerald,* 129.

53 Betty Ames Jackson. Interview with authors. St. Paul, Minnesota, 9 April 1983.

54 Kalman. Interview with Lloyd Hackl. 1975.

55 "Literary Libels: Francis Scott Key Fitzgerald," *St. Paul Daily News,* 5 March 1922, III, 6.

56 "Literary Libels: Francis Scott Key Fitzgerald," *St. Paul Daily News,* 12 March 1922, III, 6.

57 "Literary Libels: Francis Scott Key Fitzgerald," *St. Paul Daily News,* 19 March 1922, III, 6.

58 C.M. Flandrau, "Modernity—What Flandrau Heard in a Book Shop," *St. Paul Pioneer Press,* 19 March 1922, III, 8.

59 Diane Isaacs, "St. Paul's Wayward Son: Fitzgerald's Image in St. Paul Press, 1912-1945," *Conference Proceedings, F. Scott Fitzgerald: St. Paul's Son and Distinguished American Writer,* 1982, 33.

60 Cowley, *Short Stories,* 127.

61 Mayfield, *Exiles,* 80.

62 Turnbull, *Letters,* 359.

63 William Forbes, Jr. Telephone conversation with authors, 15 July 1976.

64 Mary Alice Murphy. Interview with authors. River Falls, Wisconsin, 23 April 1984.

65 Ruth Blake. Interview with authors. St. Paul, Minnesota, 25 May 1984.

66 George Muschamp. Interview with authors. St. Paul, Minnesota, 24 April 1984; F. Scott Fitzgerald, *The Vegetable* (New York: Charles Scribner's Sons, 1976), 3.

67 F. Scott Fitzgerald, *Afternoon of an Author* (New York: Charles Scribner's Sons, 1968), 185-189.

68 May Murphy. Interview with authors. St. Paul, Minnesota, 19 November 1983.

69 "Clever Lines Written by Fitzgerald for Junior League Frolic," *St. Paul Daily News,* 2 April 1922, III, 1.

70 John O'Donnell, "Fitzgerald Condemns St. Paul Flappers," *St. Paul Daily News,* 16 April 1922, 1.

71 Matthew Bruccoli, ed., *Zelda Fitzgerald: The Collected Writings* (New York: Collier Books, 1991), 387-389.

72 Bruccoli, *Zelda*, 391.

73 *Ledger*, 54.

74 Bruccoli, *Epic Grandeur*, 170.

75 Joseph H. Watson. Interview with authors. St. Paul, Minnesota, 7 July 1976.

76 Bruccoli, *Epic Grandeur*, 172.

77 Kuehl, *Dear Scott/Dear Max*, 61.

78 Mrs. Herbert L. Lewis. Letter to authors, 1 January 1977.

79 Norris Jackson. Interview at St. Paul Lexington Avenue Library. St. Paul, Minnesota, 29 October 1982.

80 Evelyn Glendenning. Interview with authors. Duluth, Minnesota, 8 September 1979.

81 Mrs. John Dalrymple. Interview with authors. Minneapolis, Minnesota, 7 September 1979.

82 Margaret Culkin Banning. Interview with authors. Brule River, Wisconsin, 22 July 1979.

83 Gene J. Marshall. Interview with authors. White Bear Lake, Minnesota, 13 August 1976.

84 Bruccoli, *Epic Grandeur*, 173.

85 Paul Maccabee, *John Dillinger Slept Here: A Crooks' Tour of Crime and Corruption in St. Paul, 1920-1936* (St. Paul: Minnesota Historical Society Press, 1995), 25.

86 Fitzgerald, *The Great Gatsby* (New York: Scribner Paperback Fiction, 1995), 127.

87 Mrs. C.J. Claude. Interview with authors. St. Paul, Minnesota, 10 November 1983.

88 Dan Runyon. Interview with authors. St. Paul, Minnesota, 28 September 1982.

89 LeVot, *Scott Fitzgerald*, 118.

Epilogue

BEFORE THE YEAR 1922 ENDED, Peggy Boyd attempted to polish out any tarnish on the image of Fitzgerald by writing a review of *Tales of the Jazz Age* for her husband's literary page in the *Daily News*. The "essential nature of Fitzgerald," she insisted, "is gay, light-hearted and pervaded with the gusto of an incorrigible love of life. . . ." Although she might have picked a less problematic comparison, Mrs. Boyd went on to say "Fitzgerald no more believes that life is meaningless than he believes in prohibition."

Mrs. Boyd confessed to liking "O Russet Witch" better than any other stories in the book, including "The Diamond as Big as the Ritz" and "May Day."[1] While today's critics might disagree with her recommendations, they would certainly support her enthusiasm, even if it was biased: At the bottom of the review, an ad appears for her book *The Love Legend*, a novel that owed its acceptance by Scribner's in large part due to Fitzgerald's intercession.

Scott may have been away from his friends, but they were not forgotten. Peggy and Thomas Boyd visited the Fitzgeralds in their Great Neck home soon after their departure from St. Paul. Donald Stewart caught up with Fitzgerald in Paris and later in Hollywood. The Kalmans visited the Fitzgeralds in Europe as well. But for the most part, Scott kept in touch through letters and had a way of popping up when least expected. When Cecil Read and

"St. Paul . . . In spite of a fifteen year absence, it still is home to me."
F. Scott Fitzgerald
to Marie Hersy,
October 28, 1936

Emily Weed were married in 1927, Scott could not attend the wedding. Several years later, the Reads received a package from Scott. The parcel was opened, and the astonished couple discovered a lovely sterling plate bearing the following inscription: TO CECIL ON THE OCCASION OF HIS MARRIAGE IN REMEMBRANCE OF 1001 MISDEEDS, SCOTT.[2]

For some of Fitzgerald's St. Paul acquaintances, Scott's transition from neighborhood friend to international celebrity took some getting used to. When the first of Fitzgerald's Basil Duke Lee stories appeared in March 1928, Scott wrote his college classmate Norris Jackson and his wife Betty to let them know he had finally included their Grand Hill home in a *Saturday Evening Post* story. Norris went out to buy the magazine and promptly placed it in a bureau drawer, unread. He was not much of a reader, he explained.[3]

After Fitzgerald's death, a large number of people interested in the author managed to find their way to 501 Grand Hill. One young lady who came to the United States from the former Yugoslavia on a Fulbright scholarship arrived at the house, and Betty asked her how she became interested in Fitzgerald. The young woman replied that *The Great Gatsby* had a particular resonance for what was happening in her native country at the time.

On another occasion, Norris was giving the Rumanian ambassador and his wife a tour of the Twin Cities. Nothing overly excited the couple's curiosity until they passed 599 Summit. "Stop

Left to right, Scottie Fitzgerald, Norris and Betty Jackson, (1982 photo by Dave Page)

the car," bellowed the ambassador's wife. "I want to get a picture." Norris was once again flabbergasted at the world-wide popularity of his friend.

In October 1964, Fitzgerald's daughter, Scottie, visited St. Paul with Mrs. Franklin D. Roosevelt, Jr., to campaign for Democratic candidates. Her first stop was the Jacksons' home on Grand Hill. Scottie commented that all the signs in the neighborhood belonged to Republicans.[4] The joke was that Betty Jackson, formerly Betty Ames, had a skeleton in her closet: she was related to Franklin D. Roosevelt.[5]

During the visit, Norris pulled out a copy of *The Beautiful and Damned* inscribed to him by the author. Scottie offered him $600 for it. "She said it was worth some money," Norris recalled. "I don't even think it went into a second printing. It wasn't that good."

AFTER HAVING MOVED to a more modest apartment near the Jacksons at 549 Grand Hill (formerly Grand Avenue), Mollie and Edward eventually followed their son out of St. Paul. Edward passed away with little fanfare in 1931 and was interred in the family plot at St. Mary's Catholic Church in Rockville, Maryland. In September 1936, Mollie was buried beside her husband. Ill, Scott could not make it to the services. In anticipation of his share of the estate, however, Scott borrowed $7,500 from Oscar and Xandra Kalman, who had remained his closest friends in St. Paul throughout his exile.

It was Oscar who was riding with Zelda in a Paris cab when she suffered her first breakdown in 1930. Later, Judy Medelman, a neighbor of the Kalmans, visited them in St. Paul. She remarked to Xandra how much she liked a painting of doves hanging on the wall. "Zelda did that," Xandra explained. Then she told the story of Zelda's hospitalization in Europe, and how she and her husband had brought her white tulips as a gift. As a thank you, Zelda, who was an incredibly talented artist, captured some doves on canvas for the Kalmans.[6]

Besides the birds, the Kalmans hung on their wall a painting by Zelda of some dancers. On September 23, 1929, Zelda had been invited to join the ballet school of the San Carlo Opera Ballet Company in Naples, Italy. Always a superb athlete, she had been offered a solo role in *Aïda* as her debut. It was a marvelous accomplishment for any woman, let alone someone pushing thirty; nevertheless, Zelda turned it down.[7]

Zelda had given the Kalmans a third painting, but Xandra found it so painful, she kept it in a closet. It was a self-portrait, largely in blue. The wrists were manacled and a baby grasps at the breast of a woman whose head is partially missing.

AFTER SCOTT DIED on December 21, 1940, James Gray of the *St. Paul Dispatch* wrote a tribute published three days later. "There can be no doubt that the Pulitzer Prize has gone to many a novel which is utterly trivial in comparison with 'The Great Gatsby,'" he eulogized. "I even venture the dreadful heresy that the Nobel prize has gone to writers for a body of work, no one item of which is as beautifully written, as revelatory of significant truths about our American psychology, as creditable in general to the level of our native intelligence and understanding as 'The Great Gatsby.'"[8] *The Daily News* had ceased publication earlier in the year; the *Pioneer Press* ran an Associated Press wire-service piece.[9]

Scott's 1937 will divided an estate "in excess of $10,000" between Zelda and Scottie. Originally, Scott wanted a "funeral and burial in keeping with my station in life," but by 1940 he had penciled out the words and written in "the cheapest funeral." The *St. Paul Dispatch* made sure to work those sentiments into an article covering Fitzgerald's death.[10] In reality, his assets amounted to approximately $35,000 after his debts were paid. His executor, Judge John Biggs, a Princeton roommate of Scott's, was able to make the amount stretch through the next seven years.[11]

Scott's meteoric rise and devastating plummet is eerily paralleled by his creation, Jay Gatz. Less than fifty copies of all Scott's works sold the year he died. Perhaps worse, he could not be interred in the family plot at St. Mary's Cemetery. An aide at the Archdiocese of Baltimore forbid the burial because Fitzgerald "had not performed his Easter duty [received Holy Communion] and his writings were undesirable."[12] A newly ordained Episcopal minister, the Reverend Raymond P. Black, said he would be willing to officiate at an alternative site since it made no difference to him who the deceased was.[13] Less than two dozen people attended the services, held on a dank day at non-denominational Union Cemetery two miles away. Zelda, claiming she did not have the strength to travel north from Alabama, was not present. Dorothy Parker, witty to the end, aptly recalled the benediction of Owl-eyes for Gatsby: "The poor-son-of-a-bitch."[14]

On the night of March 10, 1948, Zelda was sleeping at the Asheville, North Carolina, asylum where she had been undergoing treatment. A fire broke out, and nine women were killed, including Zelda. Her body was placed beside Scott's under rain-gullied, grassless earth at Union Cemetery.

On November 8, 1975, Scott and Zelda were reunited with his parents in the family plot when the Archdiocese of Washington, D.C., gained control over Rockville and gave permission for Scott to be reburied in St. Mary's Cemetery. The services were covered by Ben Franklin of the *New York Times*, whose editors quoted one of Fitzgerald's 1935 letters from Baltimore in the article's headline: "I wouldn't mind a bit if in a few years Zelda and I could snuggle up together under a stone in some old graveyard here. That is really a happy thought and not melancholy at all."[15]

WHEN SCOTT DIED, he had been away from St. Paul for over eighteen years. Many times during that hiatus he had told his friends he planned to visit, maybe next summer. In 1940, his summers ran out; but in truth he had returned to his home town countless times for material to include in his books and short stories. In fact, through his writings, he never left at all.

Notes

1 Woodward Boyd, "The Fitzgerald Legend," *St. Paul Daily News,* 10 December 1922, II, 6.

2 Emily Lu Read ne Weed. Letter to authors, 1 January 1977.

3 Norris Jackson and Betty Jackson, Interview with authors. St. Paul, Minnesota, 9 April 1983.

4 "Fitzgerald's Daughter Visits Area Birthplace," *Minneapolis Star,* 27 October 1964, 6C.

5 Louis Zelle. Interview with authors. Minneapolis, Minnesota, 5 January 1983.

6 Judy Medelman, Interview with authors. St. Paul, Minnesota, 23 April 1984.

7 Nancy Milford, *Zelda* (New York: Harper & Row, Publishers, 1970), 156.

8 James Gray, "A Last Salute to the Gayest of Sad Young Men," *St. Paul Dispatch,* 24 December 1940, 4.

9 "F. Scott Fitzgerald, Novelist, Dies," *St. Paul Pioneer Press,* 23 December 1940, 1.

10 "'Cheapest Funeral' Asked in F. Scott Fitzgerald's Will," *St. Paul Dispatch,* 22 January 1941, 7.

11 Matthew Bruccoli, *Some Sort of Epic Grandeur* (New York: Harcourt Brace Jovanovich, Publishers, 1981), 491.

12 Ben A. Franklin, "'Happy Thought' for the Fitzgeralds," *New York Times,* 8 November 1975, 29. For an excellent discussion of the controversy surrounding Fitzgerald's burial, see Joan Allen, *Candles and Carnival Light:s The Catholic Sensibility of F. Scott Fitzgerald* (New York: New York University Press, 1978), 142-144.

13 Allen, *Candles,* 143.

14 *Ibid.,* 144.

15 Andrew Turnbull, ed., *The Letters of F. Scott Fitzgerald* (New York: Dell Publishing Co., Inc., 1966), 552.

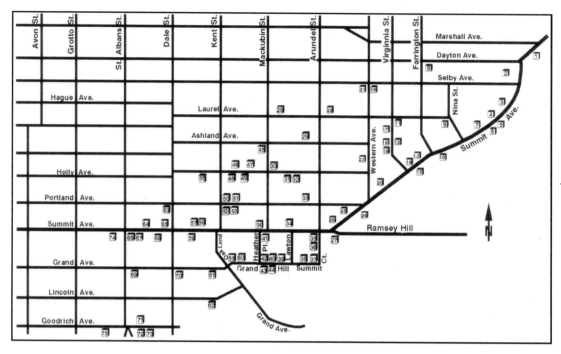

1. Josiah King Statue
2. St. Paul Cathedral
3. 239 Summit Avenue
4. 245 Summit Avenue
5. 240 Summit Avenue
6. 260 Summit Avenue
7. 251 Summit Avenue
8. 314 Dayton Avenue
9. 286, 292, & 294 Laurel Avenue, 123 Nina Avenue
10. 312 Summit Avenue
11. 130 Virginia Street
12. 96 Virginia Street
13. 335 Summit Avenue
14. 339 Summit Avenue
15. 340 Summit Avenue
16. 374 Selby Avenue
17. 121 Virginia Street
18. 107 Virginia Street
19. 89 Virginia Street
20. 365 Summit Avenue
21. 380 Selby Avenue
22. 415 Laurel Avenue
23. 79 Western Avenue
24. 400 Summit Avenue
25. 415 Summit Avenue
26. 421 Summit Avenue

27. 420 Summit Avenue
28. 481 Laurel Avenue
29. 457 Ashland Avenue
30. 499 Holly Avenue (razed)
31. 472 Holly Avenue
32. 454 Holly Avenue
33. 449 Portland Avenue
34. 475 Summit Avenue
35. 442 Summit Avenue
36. 11 Summit Court
37. 27 Summit Court
38. 33 Summit Court
39. 483 Grand Hill
40. 501 Grand Hill
41. 516 Summit Avenue
42. 511 Grand Hill
43. 514 Grand Hill
44. 506 Grand Hill
45. 79 Mackubin Street
46. 529 Holly Avenue
47. 509 Holly Avenue
48. 546 Holly Avenue
49. 514 Holly Avenue
50. Kent Street & Portland Avenue
51. 523 Portland Avenue
52. 20 North Kent Street

53. 548 Portland Avenue
54. 513 Summit Avenue
55. 561 Grand Hill
56. 580-590 Holly Avenue
57. 593 & 599 Summit Avenue
58. 587 Summit Avenue
59. 590 Summit Avenue
60. 549 Grand Hill
61. 596 Grand Avenue
62. 598 Lincoln Avenue
63. 25 North Dale Street
64. 649 Summit Avenue
65. 623 Summit Avenue
66. 676 Summit Avenue
67. 672 Summit Avenue
68. 644 Summit Avenue
69. 664-668 Grand Avenue (razed)
70 614 Grand Avenue
71. 653 Goodrich Avenue
72. 642 Goodrich Avenue
73. 626 Goodrich Avenue
74. 700 Summit Avenue
75. 708 Goodrich Avenue

Appendix

Listed below are the houses, schools, churches, clubs, and other buildings in St. Paul and White Bear Lake that are known to have F. Scott Fitzgerald connections. They are included here to facilitate walking tours along these streets. Most of the buildings are still standing; those that have been razed are so indicated. The terms "house" and "residence" are used to differentiate between those places that were more or less permanent, fixed abodes (usually owned by the person or the parents of the person who was significant in Fitzgerald's life) and those that were temporary residences, apartment houses, boardinghouses, or other less permanent dwellings. (This appendix, in slightly altered form, first appeared in F. Scott Fitzgerald in Minnesota: His Homes and Haunts by John J. Koblas, copyright 1978 by the Minnesota Historical Society. It is used with their kind permission.)

147 Summit Avenue. Thomas A. Boyd residence. He and wife, Margaret ("Peggy"), also a novelist, were friends of F. Scott. Boyd was co-owner of Kilmarnock Books, literary editor of the *St. Paul Daily News*, and author of *Through the Wheat* (1923). Razed.

226 Summit Avenue. Theodore A. Schulze house. Daughter Katharine was F. Scott's friend and a member of the Elizabethan Dramatic Club. Razed.

236 Summit Avenue. Mrs. Thomas (Jessie) Foley residence. Son

Arthur C. was a childhood friend of F. Scott. Razed.

239 Summit Avenue. John A. Fulton residence. Fulton, a physician, was a friend of Edward and Mollie Fitzgerald. They stayed briefly with him after returning to St. Paul. (See also 745 Fairmount Avenue)

240 Summit Avenue. James J. Hill house. F. Scott made reference to the Empire Builder in several of his books, including *The Great Gatsby.*

245 Summit Avenue. George R. Finch house, Violet Stockton visited Mrs. Finch, her aunt, in 1908 and had a youthful summer romance with F. Scott.

251 Summit Avenue. John R. Mitchell house, Son John ("Jack") and daughter Eleanor were friends of F. Scott. (See also 340 Summit Avenue)

260 Summit Avenue. Louis Hill house (Maryhill). Hill, son of railroad magnate James J. Hill, held parties and dances here. F. Scott sometimes attended.

312 Summit Avenue. Arthur B. Driscoll house. Sons Donald and Egbert were friends of F. Scott. This is the oldest house standing on Summit Avenue.

335 Summit Avenue. Sidney R. Stronge house. He was a friend of F. Scott. (See also 107 Virginia Avenue)

339 Summit Avenue. Charles H. F. Smith house. Son Wharton C. and F. Scott bicycled to Hastings and back during one summer.

340 Summit Avenue. John R. Mitchell house. Son John ("Jack") and daughter Eleanor were friends of F. Scott. (See also 251 Summit Avenue)

354 Summit Avenue. Silas M. Ford house. Daughter Ardietta was a childhood friend of F. Scott. Razed. (See also 511 Grand Hill)

365 Summit Avenue. C. Milton Griggs house. Benjamin G. Griggs was a friend and a classmate of F. Scott at St. Paul Academy and a member of the dancing class.

400 Summit Avenue. Lucius P. Ordway, Sr., house. Daughter Katherine was a friend of F. Scott. (See also 700 Summit Avenue)

415 Summit Avenue. William J. Dean house. Daughter Elisabeth was a close friend and confidante of F. Scott. (See also 514 Grand hill)

420 Summit Avenue. University Club. Scene of numerous dances and other festivities. Scott and Zelda published the *St. Paul Daily Dirge* for the club's "Bad Luck Ball" in 1922.

421 Summit Avenue. Charles L. Greene house. Daughter Dorothy was a friend of F. Scott and a member of the Elizabethan Dramatic Club.

442 Summit Avenue. Summit Court apartments. Mrs. Charles (Katherine K.T.) Porterfield residence and the Mrs. William Cecil (Laura) Read residence. James Porterfield and Cecil Read, two of F. Scott's closest friends, lived in this apartment building for a time. (See also 513 Summit Avenue and 449 Portland Avenue)

475 Summit Avenue. Edward L. Hersey house. Daughter Marie was one of F. Scott's closest friends during his boyhood and later when he became a successful young writer. She was probably Margaret Torrence in "The Scandal Detectives."

513 Summit Avenue. Mrs. Porterfield's boardinghouse. John DeQuedville Briggs and Donald Ogden Stewart, friends of F. Scott, briefly resided at this boardinghouse. Briggs was headmaster of St. Paul Academy. Stewart was another aspiring young writer who worked as a clerk for the telephone company while he lived in St. Paul at about the time F. Scott was completing *This Side of Paradise.*

516 Summit Avenue. Sinclair Lewis house, the "lemon meringue pie" house. Lewis rented it in October 1917 and left the following March. (See also 56 Dellwood Avenue)

540 Summit Avenue. Samuel M. Magoffin house. Daughter Elizabeth organized the Elizabethan Dramatic Club. Razed.

587 Summit Avenue. Richard ("Tubby") Washington residence. Washington, a friend since childhood, lived in the same block of row houses when F. Scott was finishing *This Side of Paradise.*

590 Summit. Avenue. Charles O. and (Sandra) Kalman house. Sandra, especially, was a close friend and a frequent rescuer of F. Scott, Zelda, and Scottie. (See also White Bear Lake)

593 Summit Avenue. F. Scott Fitzgerald residence.

599 Summit Avenue. F. Scott Fitzgerald residence. Here F. Scott polished *This Side of Paradise.*

623 Summit Avenue. Mrs. Philip F. (Louisa A.) McQuillan house. F. Scott's grandmother had this house built for herself but lived here less than three years.

644 Summit Avenue. Mrs. Gustave F. (Rose) Schurmeier house. Son Gustave B. ("Bobbie") was a close friend of F. Scott and a member of the Elizabethan Dramatic Club (See also 77 East Central)

649 Summit Avenue. The former funeral home Donald Ogden Stewart suggested vandalizing on his first meeting with F. Scott.

672 Summit Avenue. Allen and Annabel McQuillan residence. They were a brother and a sister of F. Scott's mother.

676 Summit Avenue. Allen McQuillan residence.

700 Summit Avenue. Lucius P. Ordway, Jr., house. The Ordways were friends of F. Scott.

1347 Summit Avenue. Pierce Butler house. F. Scott played with the Butler children at Frontenac in the summer of 1909.

2260 Summit Avenue. St. Paul Seminary. Father Joseph Barron, dean of the school, became a close friend and confidant of the young novelist.

11 Summit Court. Allen McQuillan residence.

27 Summit Court. Samuel D. Sturgis residence. F. Scott and Sturgis often went to matinees at the Orpheum Theatre together. (See also 123 Nina Avenue)

33 Summit Court. Reuben Warner house. Reuben was a friend and rival of F. Scott and the Hubert Blair of the Basil Duke Lee stories.

483 Grand Hill. John N. Jackson house. Son Norris was a good friend of F. Scott.

501 Grand Hill. Charles W. Ames house. Son Theodore ("Ted") and daughter Elizabeth ("Betty") were friends of F. Scott. Ames' yard was a setting for "The Scandal Detectives." Norris and Betty Jackson continued to live in the house after their marriage.

506 Grand Hill. James D. Armstrong house. Daughter Margaret was a close friend of F. Scott and probably the Imogene Bissel of "The Scandal Detectives."

511 Grand Hill. Silas M. Ford house. Daughter Ardietta was a good friend of F. Scott. (See also 354 Summit Avenue)

514 Grand Hill. William J. Dean house. Daughter Elisabeth was a good friend and confidante of F. Scott. (See aslo 415 Summit Avenue)

549 Grand Hill. Edward and Mollie Fitzgerald residence.

561 Grand Hill. Mrs. William R. (Helen T.) Dorr house. Daughter Julia was a good friend of F. Scott. She once organized an expedition to a haunted house on Pleasant. Scott "lost" Margaret Armstong to James Porterfield en route.

596 Grand Avenue. Thomas McDavitt house. Daughter Elizabeth, a member of the Elizabethan Dramatic Cloub, gave the party at which F. Scott met Ginevra King.

614 Grand Avenue. Worrell Clarkson residence. Daughter Elizabeth was a good friend of F. Scott. (See also White Bear Lake)

654 Grand Avenue. Edward P. James house. Daughter Constance was a good friend of F. Scott. Razed.

664-668 Grand Avenue. Ramaley Hall, where Professor Baker's dancing class was held. Razed.

740 Grand Avenue. Grotto Pharmacy, where Edward Fitzgerald bought his cigars. Razed.

598 Lincoln Avenue. Laurance Boardman residence. (See also 1590 Mississippi River Boulevard)

626 Goodrich Avenue. F. Scott Fitzgerald residence.

642 Goodrich Avenue. Henry J. Horn house. Daughter Margaret was a friend of F. Scott and a member of the dancing class.

653 Goodrich Avenue. Forrest Orton house. Daughter Joanne was a friend of F. Scott and a dancing class colleague. On at least one occasion, Scott went to a sleighride party she hosted.

708 Goodrich Avenue. Walter E. Alair house. Daughter Eleanor was a good friend of F. Scott. The children in Professor Baker's dancing class tried to petition her into dancing school.

720 Fairmount Avenue. Convent of the Visitation. Mollie Fitzgerald's alma mater. Scottie Fitzgerald was baptized here. Razed.

745 Fairmount Avenue. John Fulton house. (See also 239 Summit Avenue) Razed.

26 Kenwood Parkway. Philip McQuillan residence. He was an uncle of F. Scott.

449 Portland Avenue. William Cecil Read house. Son Cecil was a close friend of F. Scott and the Ripley Buckner of the Basil Duke Lee stories. The Read attic was a setting in "The Scandal Detectives" and the scene of some youthful F. Scott theatrical productions. (See also 442 Summit Avenue and White Bear Lake)

523 Portland Avenue. Lucius P. Ordway, Jr., and John Ordway house. The Ordways were friends of F. Scott.

548 Portland Avenue. Edward and Mollie Fitzgerald residence.

25 North Dale Street. St. Paul Academy. F. Scott attended the prep school for three years.

413 Holly Avenue. Austin Ballion house. Son Paul was one of F. Scott's close boyhood friends and the Bill Kempf of the Basil Duke Lee stories. Razed.

454 Holly Avenue. Charles A. Clark house. Son Robert D. ("Bob") and daughter Caroline were both friends of F. Scott.

472 Holly Avenue. Mrs. Philip F. (Louisa A.) McQuillan residence.

499 Holly Avenue. F. Scott Fitzgerald residence. Razed.

509 Holly Avenue. F. Scott Fitzgerald residence.

514 Holly Avenue. F. Scott Fitzgerald residence.

529 Holly Avenue. Paul C. Weed house. Daughter Emily Lucile, a friend of F. Scott's sister, later became Mrs. Cecil Read.

546 Holly Avenue. Dr. Benjamin H. Ogden house. Ogden was the physician who delivered F. Scott.

580-590 Holly Avenue. Mrs. Backus' School for Girls. Many of F. Scott's female friends attended the school. He took Margaret Armstrong to a dance there, and one of his theatrical productions was staged in Oak Hall.

404 Ashland Avenue. George E. Ingersoll house. Daughter Jean was a friend of F. Scott. Her mother, Janey McLaren Ingersoll, organized the dancing class. Razed.

457 Ashland Avenue. Cecil Read house. Cecil was a close friend of F. Scott. (See also 449 Portland Avenue)

286 Laurel Avenue. Laural Terrace or Riley Row. Mrs. Philip F. (Louisa A.) McQuillan residence.

292 Laurel Avenue. Daniel Mudge residence. Betty, Archie, and Dudley Mudge were friends of F. Scott.

294 Laurel Avenue. F. Scott residence. Louisa McQuillan also lived here.

415 Laurel Avenue. Charles Bigelow house. Alida and Donald were close friends of F. Scott and members of the dancing class. To Alida F. Scott wrote his famous description of 599 Summit Avenue.

481 Laurel Avenue. F. Scott Fitzgerald's birthplace.

497-499 Laurel Avenue. William H. Kane Grocery, and 500 Laurel Avenue, John Lambert's Notions. F. Scott's first outing as an infant were to these two establishments. Razed.

374 Selby Avenue. W.A. Frosts's Pharmacy, and 380 Selby Avenue, Herman W.F. Rietzke Drug (Angus Hotel). These two drugstores were occasional haunts of F. Scott when he was revising *This Side of Paradise.*

79 Western Avenue. Commodore Hotel. Scott and Zelda stayed here twice for brief periods.

514 Dayton Avenue. Ambrose Tighe house. Daughter Katherine was a good friend of F. Scott, especially in the later St. Paul years.

Dayton Avenue and Virginia Street. Aberdeen Hotel. Mollie Fitzgerald stayed here briefly after the family returned to St. Paul. Razed.

79 Mackubin Street. Edward and Mollie Fitzgerald lived here from 1893 to 1895 or 1896, then briefly at 548 Portland, before moving to 481 Laurel where Scott was born.

20 North Kent Street. Mrs. Maude Winchester residence. Daughter Margaret was a good friend of F. Scott.

Kent Street and Portland Avenue. St. John the Evangelist Episcopal Church. F. Scott made an embarrassing, drunken Christmas Eve visit to this church.

89 Virginia Avenue. Charles P. Noyes house. Son Larry was an

acquaintance of F. Scott but the latter apparently got drunk at the Noyes' house, and the two had a falling out.

96 Virginia Avenue. Charles A. Clark house, Son Robert D. and daughter Caroline were close friends of F. Scott. (See also 545 Holly Avenue)

107 Virginia Avenue. Sidney R. Stronge house. He was one of F. Scott's close friends. (See also 335 Summit Avenue)

121 Virginia Avenue. McNeil V. Seymour house. "Mac" was a close friend of F. Scott and a fellow member of the dancing class.

130 Virginia Avenue. John Townsend house. Son Theodore ("Ted") and daughter Julia were good friends of F. Scott.

123 Nina Avenue. Mrs. William Cecil (Laura) Read house. Son Cecil was one of F. Scott's closest friends. (See also 449 Portland Avenue) Samuel D. Sturgis, another friend, also lived in this row house for a time (See also 27 Summit Court)

2115 Randolph Avenue. Thomas A. Boyd residence. Razed. (See also 147 Summit Avenue.

Mississippi River Boulevard and St. Clair Avenue. Cornelius Van Ness house. Co-owner of Kilmarnock Books. Razed.

1590 Mississippi River Boulevard. Mrs. Henry A. (Cornelius Boardman house. Laurance Boardman was a good friend of F. Scott and a member of the Elizabethan Dramatic Club. He helped F. Scott get a job at the Northern Pacific carbarns.

2279 Marshall Avenue. Town and Country Club. F. Scott met Ginerva King here.

363 St. Peter Street. Hotel St. Paul. Scott and Zelda briefly stayed here.

84 East Fourth Street. Kilmarnock Books. This bookstore was a meeting place for local and visiting literary lights and F. Scott was a frequent visitor. Razed.

Sixth Street between Robert and Minnesota Streets. Metropolitan Opera House. Legitimate theater productions were given here, and in later years it was also used as a movie house. Scott and his friends probably attended both plays and movies here. Razed.

249 East Tenth Street. Philip F. and Louisa A. McQuillan house in Lower Town. Razed.

77 East Central Avenue. Mrs. Gustave F. (Rose) Schurmeier house. Son Gustave B. ("Bobbie") was a good friend of F. Scott. Razed. (See also 644 Summit Avenue)

White Bear Lake

Peninsula Road, Dellwood. William Cecil Read summer home. Cecil Read was a close friend of F. Scott. The house has been relocated. (See also 449 Portland Avenue)

14, Highway 96, Dellwood. Mackey J. Thompson home. F. Scott and Zelda lived here.

94 Dellwood Avenue. Worrell Clarkson summer home. Daughter Elizabeth and F. Scott were good friends. (See also 614 Grand Avenue)

56 Dellwood Avenue. White Bear Yacht Club. F. Scott was a frequent visitor here from boyhood on. He and Zelda lived here for a time. The clubhouse, the site of the first meeting between F. Scott and Sinclair Lewis and where F. Scott and Zelda lived, burned in 1937; a new one was built the next year.

Old Frontenac. Lake Side Hotel and Resort on Lake Pepin. Located one and one-half miles northeast of U.S. Highway 61 on Goodhue County Road 2. F. Scott spent ten days there in July 1909.

Bibliography

General Works

Allen, Joan. *Candles and Carnival Lights: The Catholic Sensibility of F. Scott Fitzgerald.* New York: New York University Press, 1978.

Andrews, General C.C. *History of St. Paul.* Syracuse, New York: D. Mason & Co., 1890.

Blegen, Theodore C. *Minnesota: A History of the State.* Minneapolis: University of Minnesota Press, 1963.

Bliss, Frank E. *St. Paul, Its Past and Present: Being an Historical, Financial, and Commercial Compendium.* St. Paul: F.C. Bliss Publishing Co., 1888.

Brown, Dee A. *Morgan's Raiders.* New York: Konecky & Konecky, 1959.

Bruccoli, Matthew. *Apparatus for F. Scott Fitzgerald's* The Great Gatsby. Columbia, South Carolina: University of South Carolina Press, 1974.

_____. *Fitzgerald and Hemingway: A Dangerous Friendship.* New York: Carroll & Graf Publishers, Inc., 1994.

_____. *Some Sort of Epic Grandeur: The Life of F. Scott Fitzgerald.* New York: Harcourt Brace Jovanovich, 1981.

_____, ed. *Zelda Fitzgerald: The Collected Writings.* New York: Collier Books, 1991.

Bruccoli, Matthew, et al., eds. *The Romantic Egoists.* New York: Charles Scribner's Sons, 1974.

Buttitta, Tony. *The Lost Summer: A Personal Memoir of F. Scott Fitzgerald.* New York: St. Martin's Press, 1987.

Callahan, John. *The Illusions of a Nation: Myth and History in the Novels of F. Scott Fitzgerald.* Urbana: University of Illinois Press, 1972.

A Century of Service to God and Man: A Brief History of the Church of St. Mary of St. Paul, Minnesota, 1867-1967. n.p.: n.d.

Cochran, Michael. "A Historical Study of the Duluth Boat Club, 1896-1926." M.A. Diss., University of Minnesota.

Davies, John. *The Legend of Hobey Baker.* Boston: Little, Brown and Company, 1966.

Donaldson, Scott. *Fool for Love.* New York: Congdon & Weed, 1983.

Drake, Carl B., et al. *The White Bear Yacht Club: Its History.* St. Paul: Bruce Publishing Co., 1961.

Empson, Donald, *The Street Where You Live.* St. Paul: Witsend Press, 1975.

Fetterley, J. "Introduction: On the Politics of Literature," from *The Resisting Reader,* 1977, in D. Herndl and R. Warhol, eds. *Feminisms: An Anthology of Literary Theory and Criticism.* New Brunswick, New Jersey: Rutgers University Press, 1991.

Fitzgerald, Zelda. *Save Me the Waltz.* New York: The New American Library, Inc., 1968.

Holmquist, June D. and Holbert, Sue E. *A History Tour of 50 Twin City Landmarks.* St. Paul: Minnesota Historical Society, 1966.

Kennedy, Roger. *Minnesota House: An Architectural & Historical View.* Minneapolis: Dillion Press, 1967.

Koblas, John J. *Sinclair Lewis: Home at Last.* Bloomington, Minnesota: Voyageur Press, 1981.

Koeper, H.F. *Historic St. Paul Buildings.* St. Paul City Planning Board, 1964.

Kriel, Margot. "Fitzgerald in St. Paul: People Who Knew Him Reminisce," in University of Minnesota Conference on F. Scott Fitzgerald, Conference Proceedings, 29-31 October 1982, pp. 21-29.

Kubista, Ivan. *This Quiet Dust: A Chronicle of Old Frontenac.* Old Frontenac, Minnesota: Old Frontenac Heritage Preservation Commission, 1978.

Kunz, Virginia B. *St. Paul: The First 150 Years.* St. Paul: The St. Paul Foundation, Inc., 1991.

Lathrop, Aaron. *Crazy Sundays: F. Scott Fitzgerald in Hollywood.* New York: The Viking Press, Inc., 1971.

Lehan, Richard. *The Great Gatsby: The Limits of Wonder.* Boston: Twayne Publishers, 1990.

LeVot, André,. *F. Scott Fitzgerald.* Garden City, New York: Doubleday, 1983.

Long, Robert, *The Achieving of The Great Gatsby: F. Scott Fitzgerald, 1920-1925.* London: Bucknell University Press, 1979.

Maccabee, Paul. J*ohn Dillinger Slept Here: A Crooks' Tour of Crime and Corruption in St. Paul, 1920-1936.* St. Paul: Minnesota Historical Society Press, 1995.

Mayfield, Sara. *Exiles from Paradise: Zelda and Scott Fitzgerald.* New York: Dell Publishing Co., Inc., 1974.

Mellow, James R. *Invented Lives: F. Scott & Zelda Fitzgerald.* Boston: Houghton Mifflin Company, 1984.

Meyers, Jeffrey. *Scott Fitzgerald.* New York: HarperCollins Publishers, 1994.

Milford, Nancy. *Zelda.* New York: Harper & Row, 1970.

Miller, James E. *F. Scott Fitzgerald: His Art and his Technique.* New York: New York University Press, 1967.

Mizener, Arthur. *The Far Side of Paradise.* New York: Avon Books, 1974.

Mizener, Arthur. *Scott Fitzgerald & His World.* Norwich, Great Britain: Jarrold & Sons, Ltd., 1972.

O'Hara, John. "Introduction," *The Portable F. Scott Fitzgerald.* New York: The Viking Press, 1945.

Piper, Henry Dan, ed. *Fitzgerald's The Great Gatsby: The Novel, The Critics, The Background.* New York: Charles Scribner's Sons, 1970.

Piper, Henry Dan. *F. Scott Fitzgerald: A Critical Biography.* New York: Holt, Rinehart, Winston, 1965.

Priestly, J.B. "Introduction," *Scott Fitzgerald.* London: The Bodley Head, 1963.

Reardon, The Rev. James M. *The Church of St. Mary of St. Paul: The Story of Pioneer Parish.* St. Paul: N.P., 1935.

Sklar, Robert. *F. Scott Fitzgerald: The Last Laocoön*. New York: Oxford University Press, 1967.

Tatar, Maria. *The Hard Facts of the Grimms' Fairy Tales*. Princeton, New Jersey: Princeton University Press, 1987.

Towne, Oliver. *St. Paul Is My Beat*. St. Paul: North Central Pub. Co., 1958.

Turnbull, Andrew. *Scott Fitzgerald*. New York: Ballantine Books, 1971.

Woolworth, Nancy L. *The White Bear Story*. White Bear Lake: N.P., 1975.

Works by Fitzgerald

Bruccoli, Matthew, ed. *As Ever, Scott-Fitz: Letters Between F. Scott Fitzgerald and His Literary Agent, Harold Ober, 1919-1940*. London: The Woburn Press, 1973.

_____. *A Life in Letters: F. Scott Fitzgerald*. New York: Simon & Schuster, 1995.

_____. *The Price was High: The Last Uncollected Stories of F. Scott Fitzgerald*. New York: Harcourt Brace Jovanovich, 1981.

Bruccoli, Matthew and Bryer, Jackson, eds. *F. Scott Fitzgerald: In His Own Time*. New York: Popular Library, 1971.

Bruccoli, Matthew and Duggan, Magaret, eds. *Correspondence of F. Scott Fitzgerald*. New York: Random House, 1980.

Broccoli, Matthew, ed. *The Notebooks of F. Scott Fitzgerald*. New York: Harcourt Brace Jovanovich, 1978.

Bruccoli, Matthew, ed. *The Short Stories of F. Scott Fitzgerald*. New York: Charles Scribner's Sons, 1989.

Bryer, Jackson R. and Kuehl, John, eds. *The Basil and Josephine Stories by F. Scott Fitzgerald*. New York: Charles Scribner's Sons, 1973.

Cowley, Malcolm. *The Stories of F. Scott Fitzgerald*. New York: Charles Scribner's Sons, 1951.

Afternoon of an Author. New York: Charles Scribner's Sons, 1957.

Babylon Revisited and Other Stories. New York: Charles Scribner's Sons, 1971.

The Crack-Up. New York: New Directions Books, 1945.

F. Scott Fitzgerald's Ledger. Washington, D.C.: NCR/Microcard Editions, 1972.

The Great Gatsby. New York: Scribner Paperback Fiction, 1995.

Taps at Reveille. New York: Charles Scribner's Sons, 1935.

This Side of Paradise. New York: Charles Scribner's Sons, 1970.

Thoughtbook of Francis Scott Key Fitzgerald. Princeton, New Jersey: Princeton University Press, 1965.

The Vegetable. New York: Charles Scribner's Sons, 1976.

Kuehl, John, ed. *The Apprentice Fiction of F. Scott Fitzgerald.* New Brunswick, New Jersey: Rutgers University Press, 1965.

Kuehl, John and Bryer, Jackson R., eds. *Dear Scott/Dear Max.* New York: Charles Scribner's Sons, 1971.

Margolies, Alan, ed. *F. Scott Fitzgerald's St. Paul Plays, 1911-1914.* Princeton, N.J.: Princeton University Library, 1978.

Turnbull, Andrew, ed. *The Letters of F. Scott Fitzgerald.* New York: Bantam Books, 1966.

Periodicals

"18 Inches of Snow and Only Five Clear Days was November Record," *St. Paul Daily News,* 2 December 1921, p. 1.

"The 'Alvina,' Beautiful New Pleasure Yacht Purchased by Thomas F. Cole," *Duluth Evening Herald,* 3 July 1909, p. 6.

"April, 1861: Minnesota Goes to War," *Minnesota History,* March 1961, pp. 212-215.

"Are at Hotel," *St. Paul Daily News,* 4 October 1921, p. 10.

"Assorted Spirits Played for Charity," *St. Paul Daily News,* 10 September 1914, p. 5.

"Boat Club Hot Weather Solace," *Duluth News Tribune,* 5 August 1909, p. 4.

Boardman, Kathryn. "F. Scott Fitzgerald's Sister Annabell [sic] Makes Final Visit to Home City," *St. Paul Pioneer Press,* 22 August 1971, pp. 27-28.

Boyd, Woodward. "The Fitzgerald Legend," *St. Paul Daily News,* 10 December 1922, II, p. 6.

"'Cheapest Funeral' Asked in F. Scott Fitzgerald's Will," *St. Paul Dispatch,* 22 January 1941, p. 7.

"Clever Lines Written by Fitzgerald for Junior League Frolic," *St. Paul Daily News,* 2 April 1922, III, p. 1.

"Cole Hidden Power in Great Mine Deals," *The New York Times,* 18 February 1906, p. 7.

"'Coward' at Y.W.C.A. Pleases a Large Crowd," *St. Paul Pioneer Press,* 30 August 1913, p. 4.

"The Daily Dirge Bemoans Failure of Cotillion on Double Jonah Day," *St. Paul Pioneer Press,* 15 January 1922, III, p. 1.

Densmore, Frances. "The Garrard Family in Frontenac," *Minnesota History,* March 1933, pp. 31-43.

Dexter, Pete. "Black Sox Blues," *Esquire,* October 1984, p. 265.

Duff, Phil. "James Hill: 'Robber barron [sic],'" *Red Wing Republican Eagle,* 13 June 1983, p. 5.

"Dust to Dust," *St. Paul Pioneer Press.* 13 April 1877, p. 4.

"F. Scott Fitzgerald is Father of Baby Girl," *St. Paul Daily News,* 27 October 1921, p. 1.

"F. Scott Fitzgerald, Novelist, Dies," *St. Paul Pioneer Press,* 23 December 1940, p. 1+

"Fitzgerald's Daughter Visits Area Birthplace," *Minneapolis Star,* 27 October 1964, p. 6C.

Flandrau, C.M. "Modernity—What Flandrau Heard in a Book Shop," *St. Paul Pioneer Press,* 19 March 1922, III, p. 8.

Forman, Elizabeth. "Santa Makes First Visit to Society Babies," *St. Paul Pioneer Press,* 25 December 1921, III, p. 1.

"Francis Key Honor Near," *St. Paul Pioneer Press,* 3 September 1914, p. 11.

Franklin, Ben A. "'Happy Thought' for the Fitzgeralds," *New York Times,* 8 November 1975, p. 29.

"Funeral of Mrs. M'Quillan," *St. Paul Pioneer Press,* 16 July 1913, p. C11.

"Girl Autoist Kills Broker," *St. Paul Pioneer Press,* 23 May 1910, p. 1+.

Gray, James. "A Last Salute to the Gayest of Sad Young Men," *St. Paul Dispatch,* 24 December 1940, p. 4.

Grey, Jane. "It's Great to be a Girl—For Three Hours Only," *St. Paul Dispatch,* 29 December 1915, p. 5.

"In a Corner with the Bookworm," *St. Paul Daily News,* 11 September, 18 September, 25 September 1921, III, p. 6.

"In Society," *St. Paul Daily News,* 23 August 1921, p. 7.

Kauffman, Michael. "Historians Oppose Opening of Booth Grave," *Civil War Times Illustrated,* June 1995, p. 28.

Keefe, Jack. "Pastoral Charm of Old Frontenac Periled by Will of the Late Owner," *Minneapolis Tribune,* 10 September 1938, p. 5.

Kent, Beth, "Fitzgerald's Back in Town," *Grand Gazette*, August 1973, p. 1+.

"Last Hint to Autoists," *St. Paul Pioneer Press*, 11 June 1910, p. 2.

"Lights Contribute Thrill to Playlet," *St. Paul Pioneer Press,* 10 September 1914, p. 12.

"Literary Libels: Francis Scott Key Fitzgerald," *St. Paul Daily News,* 5 March 1922, III, p. 6.

"The Literary Punchbowl," *St. Paul Daily News*, 15 August 1921, p. 4.

Matters, Marion. "Grandmother's House: F. Scott Fitzgerald and the Riddle of the McQuillan Residence," *Grand Gazette,* Vol. 3, No. 5, April 1976.

"More than Hundred Notes of Rejection Failed to Halt Scott Fitzgerald's Pen," *St. Paul Pioneer Press*, 12 September 1921, p. 8.

O'Donnell, John, "Fitzgerald Condemns St. Paul Flappers," *St. Paul Daily News*, 16 April 1922, p. 1.

Page, Dave. "F. Scott and Zelda in St. Paul," *City Pages*, 29 September 1982, p. 1+.

"Play Helps Babies," *St. Paul Pioneer Press*, 24 August 1912, p. 9.

"Play Nets $300 for Baby Welfare Fund," *St. Paul Pioneer Press*, 9 September 1914, p. 14.

"Readers share memories of Twin Cities railway transit," *St. Paul Pioneer Press,* 4 March 1995, p. 7A.

Roedocker, Robert L. "The Commodore Revisited," *The Grand Gazette,* Sept.-Oct. 1973, p. 1.

"Saints Drop Two Exciting Games to the Brewers at Lexington Park," *St. Paul Pioneer Press*, 23 May 1910, 6.

Schouweiler, Sara. "Minnesotan's Plane Failed," *St. Paul Pioneer Press,* 7 December 1947, p. 4.

"Scott Fitzgerald Here on Vacation; 'Rests' by Outlining New Novels," *St. Paul Daily News*, 28 August 1921, III, p. 6.

"Scott Fitzgerald Speaks at Home," *St. Paul Daily News,* 4 December 1921, II, p. 6.

Smith, Scottie Fitzgerald. "The Colonial Ancestors of Francis Scott Key Fitzgerald," *Maryland Historical Magazine*, Winter 1981, p. 375.

"Sr. Mary Helen Tells the Story of the Visitation of St. Paul," *Vision*, Spring, 1978.

"Stunning Blonde Stuns 'U' Men," *St. Paul Daily News*, 28 February 1916, 1.

"Summit Av.," *Minneapolis Star Tribune,* 9 July 1995, p. 26A.

"T.F. Cole's Yacht Due," *Duluth News Tribune,* 14 July 1909, p. 10.

"Thousands Enjoy Water Spectacle," *Duluth News Tribune,* 10 August 1909, p. 4.

"Will He Repeat?" *St. Paul Daily News,* 16 August 1921, p. 11.

Zabel, Reuben L. "Early Summit Avenue grace and elegance are part of his past," *St. Paul Dispatch,* 28 May 1979, p. 8.

Interviews

Banning, Margaret Culkin. Interview with authors. Brule River, Wisconsin, 22 July 1979.

Blake, Ruth. Interview with authors. St. Paul, Minnesota, 25 May 1 984.

Clark, Robert. Telephone conversation with authors, 18 June 1976.

Claude, Rose Snyder (Mrs. C.J.). Interview with authors. St. Paul, Minnesota, 10 November 1983.

Dalrymple, Mrs. John. Interview with authors. Minneapolis, Minnesota, 7 September 1979.

Eddy, Father Clyde. Interview with authors. St. Paul, Minnesota, 12 July 1976.

Forbes, William, Jr. Telephone conversation with authors, 15 July 1976.

Gilligan, Msgr. Francis. Interview with authors. St. Paul, Minnesota, 12 July 1976.

Glendenning, Evelyn. Interview with authors. Duluth, Minnesota, 8 September 1979.

Griggs, Benjamin. Interview with authors. St. Paul, Minnesota, 10 April 1976.

Henderson, Brooks. Interview with authors. St. Paul, Minnesota, 2 August 1976.

Jackson, Betty Ames. Interview with authors. St. Paul, Minnesota, 9 April 1983.

Jackson, Norris. Interviews with authors. 29 October 1982, 11 November 1982, 9 April 1983.

Kalman, Alexandra. Interview with Lloyd Hackl. St. Paul, Minnesota, 1975. Tape recording, Minnesota Historical Society, St. Paul, Minnesota.

Kennedy, Elisabeth Dean. Telephone conversation with authors, 15 August 1976.

Kohler, Clara. Interview with authors. St. Paul, Minnesota, 12 November 1983.

Mackenhausen, Harry. Telephone conversation with authors, 5 June 1977.

Mairs, Mr. and Mrs. George. Telephone conversation with authors, 4 June 1977.

Marshall, Gene J. Interview with authors. White Bear Lake, Minnesota, 13 August, 1976.

Mattlin, Carroll. Interview with authors. St. Paul, Minnesota, 11 December 1983.

Medelman, Judy. Interview with authors. St. Paul, Minnesota, 23 April 1984.

Murphy, Mary Alice. Interview with authors. River Falls, Wisconsin, 23 April 1984.

Murphy, May Maginnis. Interview with authors. St. Paul, Minnesota, 23 April 1984.

Muschamp, George. Interview with authors. St. Paul, Minnesota, 24 April 1984.

Osmond, Steve. Telephone conversation with authors, 25 November 1983.

Phelps, Peter B. Telephone conversation with authors, 23 April 1984.

Runyon, Dan. Interview with authors. St. Paul, Minnesota, 28 September 1982.

Schuneman, Mrs. Carl T. Telephone conversation with authors, 25 November 1977.

Stringer, Philip. Interviews with authors, August 1976; 1 March 1984.

Summersby, Jean Ingersoll. Telephone conversations with authors, 20 August 1976, 22 August 1976, 26 August 1976.

Watson, Joseph H. Interview with authors. St. Paul, Minnesota, 7 July 1976.

Zelle, Louis. Interview with authors. Minneapolis, Minnesota, 5 January 1983.

Zlonis, Dr. Mike. Telephone conversation with authors, 18 February 1984.

Correspondence

Beck, Garrard. Letter to authors, 16 December 1983.

Clark, Elizabeth Griggs. Letter to Virginia Martin, August 1978.

Clark, Robert D. Letters to authors, 24 April, 1976; 17 May 1976; 5 July 1976

Emmet, Jr., Mrs. Richard. Letter to authors, 29 March 1979.

Farrington, Mrs. John. Letter to authors, 30 November 1977.

Fitzgerald, F. Scott. Letter to Dawson Lobuston. St. Paul Public Library, St. Paul, Minnesota, 30 September 1919.

Griggs, Benjamin. Letters to authors, 13 April 1976, 28 March 1984.

Kalman, Alexandra. Letter to authors, 24 April 1984.

Labadie, Pat. Letters to authors, 1 May 1984; 3 May 1984.

Lewis, Mrs. Herbert L. Letter to authors, 1 January 1977.

Read, Clifton. Letter to authors, 3 December 1976; 8 January 1977.

Read ne Weed, (Mrs. Cecil) Emmy Lu. Letter to authors, 1 January 1977.

Sanders, Roseann. Letter to authors, 12 February 1984.

Summersby, Jean Ingersoll. Letters to authors, 12 November 1976; 20 November 1976; 4 November 1977.

Thompson, Mackey J., Jr. Letter to authors, 15 November 1976.

Index